A COLERIDGE CHRONOLOGY

AUTHOR CHRONOLOGIES

General Editor: Norman Page, Professor of Modern English
Literature, University of Nottingham

Reginald Berry
A POPE CHRONOLOGY

Edward Bishop
A VIRGINIA WOOLF CHRONOLOGY

Timothy Hands
A GEORGE ELIOT CHRONOLOGY
A HARDY CHRONOLOGY

Owen Knowles
A CONRAD CHRONOLOGY

Harold Orel
A KIPLING CHRONOLOGY

Norman Page
A BYRON CHRONOLOGY
A DICKENS CHRONOLOGY
A DR JOHNSON CHRONOLOGY
AN OSCAR WILDE CHRONOLOGY

F. B. Pinion
A KEATS CHRONOLOGY
A TENNYSON CHRONOLOGY
A WORDSWORTH CHRONOLOGY

Valerie Purton
A COLERIDGE CHRONOLOGY

J. H. Stape
AN E. M. FORSTER CHRONOLOGY

R. C. Terry
A TROLLOPE CHRONOLOGY

A Coleridge Chronology

VALERIE PURTON

M

First published 1993 by
THE MACMILLAN PRESS LTD
Houndmills, Basingstoke, Hampshire RG21 2XS
and London
Companies and representatives
throughout the world

ISBN 0–333–46021–9 hardcover

A catalogue record for this book is available
from the British Library

Printed in Great Britain by
Ipswich Book Co Ltd
Ipswich, Suffolk

Series Standing Order (Author Chronologies)

If you would like to receive future titles in this series as they are published, you can make use of our standing order facility. To place a standing order please contact your bookseller or, in case of difficulty, write to us at the address below with your name and address and the name of the series. Please state with which title you wish to begin your standing order. (If you live outside the UK we may not have the rights in your area, in which case we will forward your order to the publisher concerned.)

Standing Order Service, Macmillan Distribution Ltd, Houndmills, Basingstoke, Hampshire, RG21 2XS, England.

Contents

To my father and mother
Harry and Ella Williams

with all my love,

Val

June 1993

General Editor's Preface

Most biographies are ill adapted to serve as works of reference – not surprisingly so, since the biographer is likely to regard his function as the devising of a continuous and readable narrative, with excursions into interpretation and speculation, rather than a bald recital of facts. There are times, however, when anyone reading for business or pleasure needs to check a point quickly or to obtain a rapid overview of part of an author's life or career; and at such moments turning over the pages of a biography can be a time-consuming and frustrating occupation. The present series of volumes aims at providing a means whereby the chronological facts of an author's life and career, rather than needing to be prised out of the narrative in which they are (if they appear at all) securely embedded, can be seen at a glance. Moreover, whereas biographies are often, and quite understandably, vague over matters of fact (since it makes for tediousness to be forever enumerating details of dates and places), a chronology can be precise whenever it is possible to be precise.

Thanks to the survival, sometimes in very large quantities, of letters, diaries, notebooks and other documents, as well as to thoroughly researched biographies and bibliographies, this material now exists in abundance for many major authors. In the case of, for example, Dickens, we can often ascertain what he was doing in each month and week, and almost on each day, of his prodigiously active working life; and the student of, say, *David Copperfield* is likely to find it fascinating as well as useful to know just when Dickens was at work on each part of that novel, what other literary enterprises he was engaged in at the same time, whom he was meeting, what places he was visiting, and what were the relevant circumstances of his personal and professional life. Such a chronology is not, of course, a substitute for a biography; but its arrangement, in combination with its index, makes it a much more convenient tool for this kind of purpose; and it may be acceptable as a form of 'alternative' biography, with its own distinctive advantages as well as its obvious limitations.

Since information relating to an author's early years is usually scanty and chronologically imprecise, the opening section of some volumes in this series groups together the years of childhood and adolescence. Thereafter each year, and usually each month, is dealt with separately. Information not readily assignable to a specific month or day is given as a general note under the relevant year or month. The first entry for each month carries an indication of the day of the week, so that when necessary this can be readily calculated for other dates. Each volume also contains a bibliography of the principal sources of information. In the chronology itself, the sources of many of the more specific items, including quotations, are identified, in order that the reader who wishes to do so may consult the original contexts.

NORMAN PAGE

Introduction

There are many accounts of Coleridge's life, including the one he presented himself in his conversations with James Gillman, in which the lonely Bluecoat boy abandoned by his family is the romantic central figure. The present chronology serves to demythologise that figure by revealing the support the young Coleridge received from his uncle's family and from two of his elder brothers during his London schooldays. Dickens in a very similar way was to present to Forster the story of the friendless young lad sold to the blacking factory. A powerful sense of exclusion and isolation was for both writers a constant source of inspiration and it is one function of chronology to track that notion to its historical source. There are many things a chronology cannot do: it can give only a sketchy outline of the complexities of Coleridge's dealings with his assorted publishers; it can only touch on the vexed issue of plagiarism so thoroughly adumbrated by Norman Fruman; it can merely suggest the nature of subtle relationships with Wordsworth, Sara Hutchinson and others; but it can, perhaps better than other forms of biography, give the warp and woof of 62 years in which life and works are intricately and suggestively linked. It is possible, for example, to see Coleridge, on 3 November 1810, scribbling a note on the manuscript of 'Kubla Khan' to the effect that its composition was the result of recourse to opium at the height of the quarrel with Charles Lloyd – a comment which led E. H. Coleridge and others to re-date the poem's genesis from autumn 1797 to summer 1798. However, there were particular reasons on 3 November 1810 for Coleridge to be thinking painfully about lost friendship and betrayal: he had that very day taken refuge with the Morgan family after the shock of Wordsworth's 'betrayal' of him to Basil Montagu (which was to remain one of the four 'griping and grasping Sorrows' of his life). The physician Anthony Carlisle had that month been spreading rumours about his opium habit and Morgan had himself fed STC's sense of persecution by speaking of enemies at work against his character. No wonder, then, that the supreme opium vision of more than a decade before should merge in his memory with that earlier, lesser act of betrayal by Lloyd, regardless of its actual date of composition.

There are, of course, strong arguments *against* a biographical approach to Coleridge – and they are expressed particularly well by his own son:

> It is thought by many that the lives of literary men are sufficiently known from their writings, and that any record of their private history is at best superfluous. Much may be said in support of this opinion. Of poets more especially it may be affirmed, that the image which they put forth of themselves in their works is a true and adequate representation of the author, whatever it may be of the man: nay, that in many cases it may depict the man more faithfully, – may show more truly what he was, than any memorial of what he did and suffered in his mortal pilgrimage, too often a sad tissue, so it is made to appear, of frailty and sorrow.[1]

Derwent Coleridge is here thinking of his brother Hartley, but what he says applies with even more force perhaps to his father, and should certainly give pause to the boldest biographer, let alone the humble chronologist. However, Derwent's later justification for his memoir of Hartley, that it is designed to 'save the memory of a departed friend or relative from misrepresentation', is enough to give one heart. No great writer has suffered more from misrepresentation than STC. In his lifetime his ability to evoke loyalty and even adoration was matched only by his propensity for being misunderstood, particularly by his closest friends and family. The myth of the weak-willed, self-absorbed opium addict, the 'damaged arch-angel', can perhaps be dispelled more readily by that day-to-day compilation of actions which is the field of the chronologist than by the subtler but necessarily more subjective skills of the biographer.

One example among many is the manner in which literary history has recorded the bankruptcy of STC's old friend John Morgan, whose loyalty and kindness rescued Coleridge in the depths of his drug addiction in 1810 and whose work as an amanuensis continued well into the Highgate years. Southey, an old school-friend of Morgan's, writes to Joseph Cottle in February 1836: 'I will tell you what John Morgan said to me the last time I ever saw him. He said that he never knew any man could bear the misfortunes of his friends with more indifference than Coleridge! They were cut to the heart by his utter neglect of them after their ruin.'[2] The chronologist, however, records that during 1813 STC pawned his books, raised £100 for Morgan's creditors, demanded letters from Mrs Morgan every other day to satisfy him about her state of health, and arranged a retreat in Wiltshire for her and for her sister Charlotte; that he was caring for the family in 1819 when Morgan suffered the severe stroke which led to his death; and that as late as 1828 he was writing to friends to raise £20 for the widow and her sister.

There is, from this and many other examples, a special justification for a chronology of Coleridge the man; a more worrying question is that of the relevance of such an undertaking to an understanding of Coleridge the poet. Here there is more involved than Derwent's strictures about the self-sufficiency of the works themselves, an argument which applies with equal force to all great writers: with STC there is a much greater difficulty. What is the chronologist to do about the huge dim shadowland of unrealised and unrealisable dreams and projects in which this particular writer spent his days? What E. K. Chambers calls Coleridge's 'Literary aircastles' exasperated friends and publishers in his lifetime and have tried the patience of scholars ever since. Even the magisterial E. L. Griggs, after editing a long series of STC's letters filled with ever-more-detailed plans of his forthcoming book on the German expedition, finally snaps in a testy footnote, 'It is worth remarking once for all that Coleridge did not publish a German tour' (*Letters*, I. 655n.). Coleridge's shadowland contains such unwritten works as 'Imitations from the Modern Latin Poets' (1794), 'The Progress of Liberty, on the Visions of the Maid of Orleans' (1797), 'The Brook' (1797), 'The Life of Lessing' (begun in 1798 and still in the air in 1800), the 'Logosophia' (1815), an epic on the destruction of Jerusalem (1818), and of course the Opus Maximum, over the notes for which the loyal J. H. Green struggled until his death. I have tried to record such invisible works wherever possible and in the later years, when the life of the mind, manifest in conversation with his friends and followers, was even more obviously the best part of STC's 'real' life, I have borrowed freely from H. N. Coleridge's *Table Talk* (which has the additional virtue of reasonably accurate dating). Throughout, I have borne in mind Kathleen Raine's caveat:

No life suffers more than Coleridge's from any attempt to reduce it to the personal level. Flashes of poetic vision, the deep soundings of metaphysical intuition and of spiritual revelation – these were the real events . . . [3]

In order to shape this record of 62 years as a reference tool I have had to reduce the richness and exuberance of those years into a manageable form; in doing so I am all too aware of the omissions and simplifications that have been necessary. I have, for example, given little detail about the contents of the *Watchman* and the *Friend*, since that information is readily available elsewhere. On the other hand, I have included apparently trivial details of daily movements from the Alfoxden and Grasmere Journals, in an effort both to pin STC down to earth and to show the diurnal reality of his constant contact with the Wordsworths. (Surely it is only a matter of time before some over-assiduous biographer calculates the mileage involved in the production of the *Lyrical Ballads*)

References in the text have been kept to a minimum. Letters are almost always identifiable by the name of the recipient and the date and extra information is supplied only where absolutely necessary. The Bibliography directs the reader to the relevant letters or journals of each major figure. Such a study as this can usefully clear up minor confusions which belong to early biographers and have been inherited by later ones. One such is the tradition (adopted by W. Jackson Bate and recently by Richard Holmes, among others) about the surname of the kindly shoemaker who braved the wrath of James Bowyer in 1787 in an attempt to rescue young Sam from the rigours of Christ's Hospital. He appears in most Coleridgean indexes as 'Mr Crispin'. It seems to me obvious, from a glance at the original reference in Gillman, that STC and Gillman were simply using the generic term for a shoemaker in a Christian society – St Crispin being the patron saint of that profession.

One of the most useful techniques available to the chronologist is that of juxtaposition. S/he can be in several places at once – following STC to Malta, for example, while watching the effect of his prolonged absence on the family at home. I make no apologies for including in a Coleridge chronology the reactions of those closest to him. Especially poignant are the parallel entries for 1798, when STC was lost in German philosophy in Göttingen while his wife in Bristol watched baby Berkeley sicken and die of consumption. The gulf between the two on STC's return, which was to have such a profound effect on his life and on his work, is much more explicable if one has, in Richard Holmes's phrase, followed the participants' 'living footsteps through the world' and seen events as they saw them at the time. Whenever it has seemed more helpful to the reader, however, I have also exploited hindsight: in October 1800, for example, to point out that Wordsworth's rejection of 'Christabel' was final; he did not, as he suggested to STC at the time, publish it later with his own poem, 'The Pedlar'. (I have used square brackets to indicate such intrusions of, as it were, an 'omniscient narrator'.)

A more sinister juxtaposition in 1832 reveals that on 6 January Coleridge sent out his usual request to T. H. Dunn, the Highgate chemist, to have a bottle filled with 'Tinct. Op.', the inevitable opium. During the year, however, letters to J. H. Green and H. F. Cary speak of a 'miracle of grace' which has released him from '33 years' fearful Slavery' to the drug. After being with him at the christening of their second grandchild, Edith, in August, Mrs Coleridge writes to Poole that her husband 'has entirely left off the use of opium'. Yet in December comes the familiar request to Dunn – suggesting that Coleridge's abstention was closer to wishful thinking than reality.

Coleridge's charm was legendary: it captivated poets and politicians, the powerful and the weak, the old and the young. As a schoolboy he cannoned into an elderly gentleman in the Strand who at first thought of arresting him as a pickpocket, but soon succumbed and set him up with a ticket for a lending library. As an old man (in health if not in years), he was adored by his youthful disciples, who asked his advice on their love affairs as well as on intellectual matters. He wrote the last letter of his life to his infant godchild, Adam Steinmetz; his final act before lapsing into a coma was to scribble a note asking for a legacy to be raised for his faithful servant, Harriet Macklin. It is too much to expect that a chronology of Coleridge could be objective. A photographer has to choose where to point a camera and a historian has to choose which information to highlight and which to ignore. At the same time, as Larkin puts it, 'Days are where we live' – and it is in the recording of those days as accurately as possible *as they occurred* that the chronologist hopes to enable the subject to speak for himself.

Notes

1. Derwent Coleridge, *Memoir of Hartley Coleridge*, 1851, p. xiii.
2. *New Letters of Robert Southey*, ed. Kenneth Curry (New York: Columbia University Press) vol. 2, p. 443.
3. Kathleen Raine, Introduction to *Selected Letters* (London: Grey Walls Press, 1950) p. ix.

The Coleridge Family

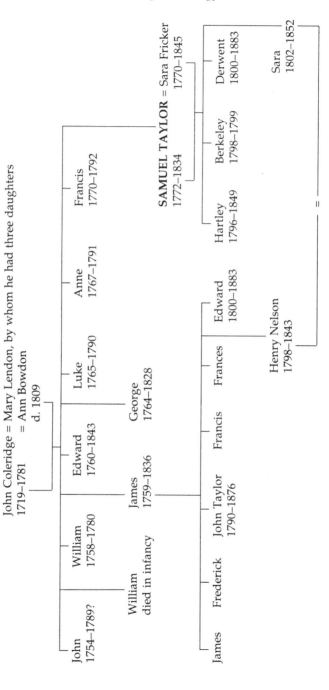

John Coleridge = Mary Lendon, by whom he had three daughters
1719–1781   = Ann Bowdon
             d. 1809

John
1754–1789?

William
1758–1780

William
died in infancy

Edward
1760–1843

James
1759–1836

George
1764–1828

Luke
1765–1790

Anne
1767–1791

Francis
1770–1792

SAMUEL TAYLOR = Sara Fricker
1772–1834   1770–1845

Hartley
1796–1849

Berkeley
1798–1799

Derwent
1800–1883

Sara
1802–1852

James

Frederick

John Taylor
1790–1876

Francis

Frances

Edward
1800–1883

Henry Nelson
1798–1843

=

Reproduced from Allan Grant's *A Preface to Coleridge* (London: Longman, 1972) by kind permission of the author.

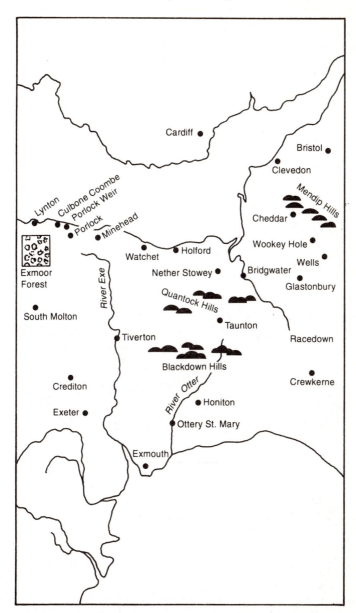

Map 1   Parts of Devon and Somerset

Source: Maps 1–4 are reproduced from Allan Grant's *A Preface to Coleridge* (London: Longman, 1972) by kind permission of the author.

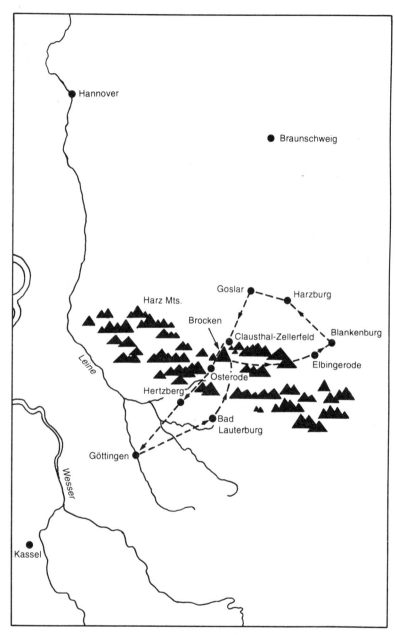

*Map 2   Harz district of Germany
showing Coleridge's walking tour of 1799*

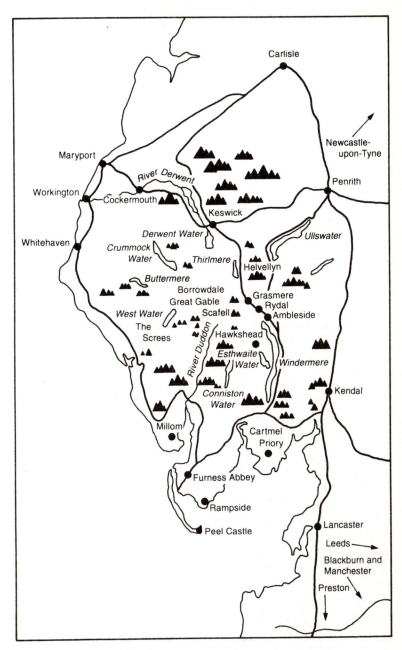

Map 3   The Lake District

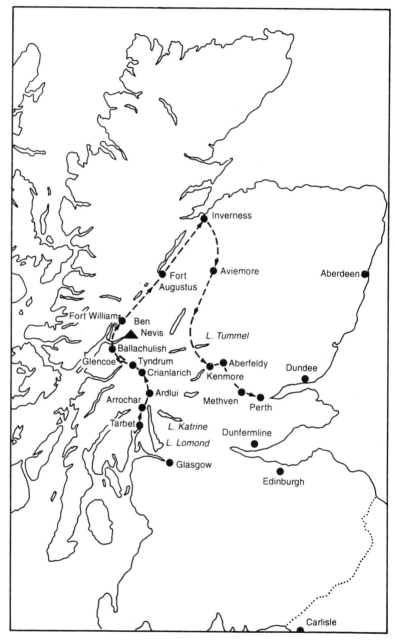

Map 4   Coleridge's Scottish walk of 1803

List of Abbreviations

The abbreviation STC throughout refers to Samuel Taylor Coleridge. This is particularly appropriate, as it was his own favoured acronym and he used it, often in the Greek form, ΕΣΤΗΣΕ, as a signature for letters. Other abbreviations, set out below, are used frequently, except where a personal reference seems needed.

Persons

CL	Charles Lamb
DW	Dorothy Wordsworth (WW's sister)
HCR	Henry Crabb Robinson
HNC	Henry Nelson Coleridge (STC's nephew)
Mrs C	Sara Coleridge (STC's wife)
MW	Mary Wordsworth (WW's wife)
RS	Robert Southey
Sara H	Sara Hutchinson
WW	William Wordsworth

Publications

BL	*Biographia Literaria*
LB	*Lyrical Ballads*

A Coleridge Chronology

Early Years (1772–81)

STC's grandfather, John Coleridge, was 'dropped as a child' in the Hundred of Coleridge in Devon, 'christened, educated and apprenticed by the parish', but overcame his humble beginnings to become a respectable woollen draper in Crediton. (STC himself always thought it was South Molton.) STC delighted, at the time of the French Revolution, in claiming that his grandfather had been a workhouse bastard, and on one occasion claimed the same for his father; however, John Coleridge the younger was in fact sent to the local grammar school where he held an exhibition and where he stayed until his father's bankruptcy when John was sixteen. The boy was then helped by a friend, James Buller of Downes near Crediton, to become a schoolmaster in a neighbouring village, Clyst Hydon. He married Mary Lendon of Crediton, by whom he had four daughters. STC himself mentions only three: Mary (became Mrs Bradley); Sarah (married a seaman and died young); and Elizabeth (brought up with the children of the second marriage; she became Mrs Jacob Phillips of Exeter). In 1747, at the age of 28, John had saved up enough money to enter Sidney Sussex College, Cambridge, where he distinguished himself in Hebrew and mathematics. He left before taking his degree, in 1749, to become headmaster of Squire's Grammar School at South Molton and curate of nearby Mariansleigh. His first wife died in 1751 and in 1754 he married Ann Bowdon, daughter of an Exmoor farmer. In 1760 he became headmaster of the King Henry VIII Grammar School at Ottery St Mary and also vicar of St Mary's; here he remained until his death in 1781.

Ann Bowdon came of a respectable farming family which, said STC, 'had inherited a small farm in the Exmoor county in the reign of Elizabeth'. The couple had ten children:

John (1754–89) Went to the East Indies for the East India Company and thence to India; it seems that he never saw STC, but he concerned himself about the boy's career, even suggesting that he

1

join him in India as a cadet. This was prevented by John's death at Tillicherry from malaria.

William: died in infancy.

William (1758–80) Went to Pembroke College, Oxford, then taught in Hackney. He died of 'a putrid fever' on the eve of his marriage to Jane Hart of Exeter.

James (1759–1836) Joined the army at sixteen; he became a lieutenant-colonel and eventually married an heiress, Frances Taylor; he lived grandly in Ottery in the Chantry House. He was the father of Henry Nelson Coleridge, who married STC's daughter Sara.

Edward (1760–1843) 'The Wit of the family', went to Pembroke College, Oxford. He became a clergyman and married, said STC, 'a woman twenty years older than my mother'.

George (1764–1828) STC's favourite brother. He went to Pembroke College, Oxford, then took William's place at Mr Newcombe's School in Hackney. In 1796 he married William's former fiancée, Jane Hart. 'He is worth the whole family in a lump', said STC. He followed his father and took the living and the headmastership at Ottery St Mary.

Luke Herman (1765–90) Trained as a doctor and married Sara Hart. He became the father of William Hart Coleridge, Bishop of Barbados.

Anne (1767–91) Beloved 'Nancy', who died of consumption.

Francis Syndercombe (1770–92) 'The handsome Coleridge'. He went as a midshipman to India, where he by chance met his brother John, who procured for him a commission in the army. He fought bravely at Seringapatam and was presented with a gold watch by his commanding officer; however, he contracted a fever there and in a delirium shot himself.

Samuel Taylor Born 21 October 1772 'at eleven o'clock in the forenoon'. (He always thought of his birthday as the 20th.) He was christened after a godfather, Samuel Taylor Esq. of Ottery, and had another godfather, Mr Evans, and two godmothers, both called Mundy.

As the youngest, STC seems to have been a favourite child. In his second year, when his nurse carelessly left him by the fire, he pulled out a live coal and 'burnt myself dreadfully'. While having his hand dressed, he spoke his first words, according to his mother: 'Nasty Dr Young!'

As a small child he went to 'Old Dame Key's' school (she was a relation of Sir Joshua Reynolds) and by the age of three 'could read a chapter in the Bible'. From October 1775 to October 1778 he 'continued at the Reading School'. His parents' darling, he inevitably attracted the jealousy of his older brothers, particularly of the lively, outgoing Frank, whose envy was encouraged by their nursemaid, Molly. Driven in upon himself by his exclusion from the play of the boys at school, he read the more avidly, fairy tales and the *Arabian Nights* being his favourites. His father, troubled by Sam's intense imagination, finally burnt these overstimulating books. By the time he went to his father's grammar school in October 1778, STC was already 'a character', beloved of adults but disliked by his peers, physically lazy, intellectually precocious. In the first week of October 1780, a fierce quarrel with Frank sent the emotional child rushing out into the countryside, where he stayed all night on the banks of the River Otter, full of gloomy satisfaction at the thought of 'how miserable my mother must be'. After most of the villagers had searched for him all night, he was discovered at five in the morning by Sir Stafford Northcote, the local landowner; he remembered ever afterwards the delight of his parents when he was carried home. (This incident remained with him all his life; see, for example, stanza seven of 'Dejection'.) In his first year at the grammar school (1779), Sam and his brother George both fell victim to an epidemic of 'putrid fever' and were isolated in the school house. During this time Sam grew closer to George, whom he later saw as a 'second father'. Frank too would creep in and read Pope's *Homer* to him. He came to idolise his only sister, Nancy, but his feelings about his mother were increasingly ambivalent, and later in life he felt that she had rejected him. All his life, however, he adored the memory of his father, whom he saw as a simple, unworldly scholar. (He had published several academic textbooks and contributed to the *Gentleman's Magazine*.) His father was certainly central to his early intellectual development, encouraging his reading in the hope that he would one day enter the Church, and teaching him, too, about the stars and the planets.

1781

October
4   (Thurs) John Coleridge returns home from Plymouth, where he has settled Francis, aged twelve, as a junior midshipman under Admiral Graves, a family friend, who is setting out with

a convoy for Bengal. He tells his family (apart from STC, not quite nine, who is in bed) of a vivid dream of Death which he has had the previous night. During the night he dies suddenly of a heart attack. Woken by his mother's shriek, STC cries out 'Papa is dead!' The family have to move out of the Vicarage and School House into the Warden's House nearby, lent to them by Sir Stafford Northcote.

1782

STC continues temporarily as a day-boy at the grammar school, without paying fees, under his father's successor, Parson Warren, whom he thinks is 'a booby'. Mrs Coleridge cannot afford school fees. Plans for sending STC to Charterhouse fall through. Judge Francis Buller, a former pupil of John Coleridge and son of his benefactor, James Buller, recommends that the family apply to Christ's Hospital, London, founded for the sons of needy clergy.

March
28   (Thurs) Samuel Taylor, STC's godfather, draws up a petition for him to Christ's Hospital, countersigned by the new vicar, the Reverend Fulwood Smerdon. This petition gives the school authorities the right to apprentice the boy if he does not prove academically promising. [Brother John in India objects to this and sends £200, telling James not to neglect Sam's education and strongly urging that Nancy should not (as is planned) be sent to work as a shop-assistant at a milliner's in Exeter.]

April
STC is accepted by Christ's Hospital, probably at the instigation of Judge Buller and with the help of John Way, one of the school's governors. He is sent immediately to stay with his maternal uncle, John Bowdon, who works as a tobacconist and part-time clerk to an underwriter, in Threadneedle Street in London. He is there for ten weeks and is taken to taverns and coffee houses by his uncle, where he astonishes the company with his conversation. He is regarded as a prodigy. The family consists of his uncle, an 'ugly and an artful' daughter, Betsy, and a Miss Cabriere, 'an old Maid of great sensibilities & a taste for Literature'. There seems also to have been a married sister of Bowden's, Mrs Short, and her children.

July

8   (Mon) STC is enrolled at Christ's Hospital junior school, Hertford, for six weeks. Here, as with his uncle, he is happy and has plenty to eat.

September

He arrives at Christ's Hospital in London and is placed in Jefferies' Ward in the Under-Grammar School, run by the Reverend Matthew Field. STC later in life stresses his sense of utter isolation from his family. [See 'Frost at Midnight', 'Dejection: an Ode' and also references to STC in WW's 'Prelude', vi. 274 and CL *Works*, ii. 13. However, there is evidence of visits home (see February 1785).] Field is not a disciplinarian, but STC is still miserable in the harsh school regime. The food is bad and STC's health seems already precarious.

Sir Francis Buller, STC's patron and now a High Court Judge, invites him regularly to dine with his family on Sundays – until one day he is placed at the second table. The boy's pride is hurt so badly that he never returns.

At some time during these early years, on his wanderings on 'whole-day-leaves' around London, STC encounters in the Strand a kindly old gentleman who at first mistakes him for a pickpocket, but later gives him a ticket for the lending library in King Street nearby. From then on, he reads voraciously 'through the catalogue, folios and all, whether I understood them or did not understand them'.

1784

May

7   (Fri) Tom Evans enters the school and is befriended by STC, who later makes friends with his whole family.

STC's earliest poems are rhymes to ward off schoolboy ailments. He already enjoys magical incantations.

October

5   (Tues) STC's brother Luke is admitted to study to be a surgeon at the London Hospital. [STC visits him regularly on Saturdays and becomes fascinated by medicine.]

1785

This year, STC's brother George comes down from Oxford and teaches at Newcome's Academy in Hackney.

February

4 (Fri) A letter to his mother thanking her for gifts from home talks of recently seeing brother Luke and shows that STC is still being cared for by his uncle and family. It also shows him still closely in touch with friends at Ottery, suggesting recent visits. [This all belies his own later accounts of complete friendlessness and isolation during these years.]

Probably during this year, an Upper School boy, Thomas Fanshawe Middleton, one day finds STC reading Virgil for pleasure and brings him to the attention of the Headmaster, the Reverend James Bowyer, a stern but efficient teacher and a great flogger. Deciding that the boy is to become a Grecian (the academic élite of the school who are destined for Oxford and Cambridge), Bowyer thrashes him to remind him to work hard. (Field has described him as being dull and lazy in class.) STC later describes himself at that time as an ugly boy with a shock of black hair, and recounts that Bowyer would give him an extra stroke when flogging him, 'because you are such an ugly fellow!' Finding the boy in tears once after a visit home, Bowyer shouts, 'Boy! the school is your father! Boy! the school is your mother!'

1787

February

STC enters the Upper School. Life under Bowyer is so hard that on one occasion he tries to get himself apprenticed to a shoemaker whom he persuades to visit the Headmaster to claim him. Bowyer chases the man from the room and knocks the boy down. [However, much later STC eulogises Bowyer in the *BL Supplement*: he values his stress on the best classical authors and on Shakespeare and Milton, and his insistence that 'Poetry . . . has a logic of its own, as severe as that of science.' For sterner assessments of Bowyer, see CL and Leigh Hunt.]

May
Luke Coleridge has left London to set up a medical practice at Thorverton, near Exeter.

12 (Sat) STC writes to congratulate Luke and sends him his first serious poetry, six stanzas on 'Easter Holidays' and a Latin translation on the subject of loneliness and misery, 'Nil pejus est caelibe vita'. Bowyer later accepts the latter for inclusion in the school's 'Album' and promises that STC will become a deputy Grecian within a year if he works hard.

The Bowdons are still caring for STC: he dines there every Saturday and Betsy and Miss Cabriere are particularly kind to him. There is also his brother George, who is, he says, 'father, brother and everything to me'.

1788

STC becomes a 'Grecian'. He reads Cato's *Letters* and Voltaire's *Philosophical Dictionary*, and 'for a few months became an infidel', until Bowyer finds out and flogs him severely. [STC later describes this as 'the only just flogging I ever had from him'.] He reads Edward Young's 'Night Thoughts', which he had requested from Luke the previous year.

He visits the home of Tom Evans in Villiers Street off the Strand and there meets the widowed Mrs Evans, who becomes his mother-substitute, and her three daughters, Mary, Anne and Elizabeth. 'Of course I fell in love with the eldest.' For the next three years he spends Saturdays with the family and is thrilled to escort the Miss Evanses home.

1789

May
26 (Tues) STC writes to brother George asking for a new pair of breeches, if possible before Whitsunday; his present pair 'are not altogether so well adapted for the female eye'.

Jul

14   (Tues) The Fall of the Bastille and the beginning of the French Revolution. STC writes a long poem to commemorate the event.

August

STC visits Ottery. Carves his initials at entrance of the cave known as the Pixies' Parlour. Finds out that his beloved sister Anne (Nancy) is dangerously ill with consumption.

September

He writes a sonnet, 'Life', about his sister's illness. Some time in the autumn he writes 'To the Autumnal Moon'. At this period, too, STC and other boys swim in the River New at Newington fully clothed and let their clothes dry on them. This puts STC in the school hospital for several weeks with jaundice and fever, and seems to mark the beginning of his life-long tendency to rheumatic ailments. He writes a sonnet, 'Pain', about his illness and a love poem, 'Genevieve', about the young woman who nurses him. [See letter to Richard Sharp, 18 December 1807, asking for help for a nurse at Christ's Hospital.]

Thomas Middleton, now at Jesus College, Cambridge, sends STC a copy of the second edition of William Lisle Bowles's *Sonnets*. STC is enraptured. (Perhaps their emotional modernity is a relief after Bowyer's classical taste?) During the next eighteen months he writes out 40 copies of the poems to give to friends.

This year Bowyer accepts from STC for inclusion in the Christ's Hospital 'Album' a poem in the style of Pope, 'Julia' and a Latin translation, 'Quae nocent docent'. STC's friends at this time include Robert Allen (who shares his visits to the Evans family), Charles Valentine Le Grice and his younger brother Samuel, Samuel Favell, John Matthew Gutch and Frederick William Franklin. [He also knows Charles Lamb, but the friendship does not blossom until they meet again in London in 1794.]

1790

During this year STC writes 'On Receiving an account that his only Sister's Death was Inevitable'. The earliest version of 'Monody on the Death of Chatterton' is published in the Christ's Hospital 'Album'. He also writes and sends to George a parody of Bowles's 'Monody on a Tea-kettle'.

December
(late)   Luke Coleridge dies suddenly in Exeter of a fever.

1791

January
12   (Mon) STC is granted a Christ's Hospital Exhibition worth £40, renewable for four years.

February
5   (Fri) He is elected to a sizarship at Jesus College, Cambridge, with a promise of a Rustat Scholarship of £30 (reserved for sons of clergymen who show outstanding merit).
During this month or the next, STC sends George a Latin Ode in honour of A. W. Trollope, who has been awarded the Chancellor's Medal.

March
Anne Coleridge dies of consumption. STC writes 'On Seeing a Youth Affectionately Welcomed by a Sister' (this is probably Tom Evans).
31   (Thurs) He sends George a Pindaric ode on Euclid's geometry, and comments on Mathematics that, 'though Reason is feasted, Imagination is starved'.

May
17   (Tues) He writes to George that a sore throat has delayed his letter-writing.

June
22   (Wed) He sends two poems to George, 'Happiness' and 'Life' (from 1789) about Anne's illness.

August
17   (Wed) On his way home to Ottery he writes 'In the Coach'.
18   Later on the same journey, he writes 'Devonshire Roads'; he

has left the coach at Plymtree, eight miles from Ottery, to walk home.

September
7   (Tues) STC's formal discharge from Christ's Hospital. He writes 'Sonnet: On Quitting School for College' ('Farewell, parental scenes! A sad farewell!').

October
16   (Sat) STC goes up to Cambridge.

November
He writes to George of his new routine: chapel twice a day; mathematics lectures which he enjoys; classics lectures not yet begun but apparently poorly attended.
28   (Mon) Opium makes its first appearance in a letter to George. STC is taking it to alleviate the rheumatism brought on by the damp Cambridge climate: 'Opium never used to have any disagreeable effect on me – but it has upon many.'
He spends much time with Thomas Middleton, his old schoolfellow, now at Pembroke. He has a good friend, too, in George Caldwell.

December
STC spends a fortnight over Christmas with the Evans family. Mrs Evans nurses him back to health and his attachment to her grows.

1792

January
24   (Tues) STC sends George a sermon to deliver. (He is apparently used to preparing sermons for his brother.) George is worried to hear that STC has made the acquaintance of William Frend, Fellow of Jesus, who is a Unitarian.

February
6   (Mon) STC's brother Francis is wounded at the Battle of Seringapatam and shortly afterwards shoots himself in a delirium. [STC does not hear the news for a year.]

13 STC writes affectionately to Mrs Evans, sending her a poem, 'To Disappointment'. He sends his compliments to 'Mr Tomkyns' [see 2 December 1793]. He sends Mary, in a joky, flirtatious letter, 'An Ode in the Manner of Anacreon' and 'A Wish written in Jesus Wood Feb 10 1792'.

April

2 (Mon) STC tells George that he means to work for all the university prizes, the Greek Ode, the Latin Ode and the Epigrams, although 'I have little or no expectation of success.' He sends George another sermon.

He has fallen into the Cam while boating for the first time, but seems to be none the worse.

June

STC's Greek Sapphic ode on the slave trade wins the Sir William Browne Gold Medal.

16 (Sat) He sends an autograph copy of the ode to brother George.

July

3 (Tues) STC declaims the ode before all the Fellows at the Encaenia. He then goes to the Evans family in London and becomes increasingly infatuated with Mary.

11 (Wed) STC visits his brother Edward in Salisbury (he is assistant master at Dr Skinner's school), and finds him as witty as ever (suffering from 'Punnomania').

16 He moves on to visit brother James in Exeter.

August

During this month STC visits his half-sister Mrs Phillips at Tiverton and his mother at Ottery. He does not enjoy their company, nor that of his brothers, and tells George that the Devon visit has 'annihilated whatever tender ideas' he had preserved of the place.

24 (Fri) He writes to George from Ottery (in Latin) that their mother complains about her poor health more than usual. The letter is full of gossip about local people, suggesting that he must have kept in touch with them during his years at school.

During the Michaelmas term STC becomes involved in political and literary discussions, supporting the cause of Frend and joining in the excitement at the development of events in the French Revolution.

November

11 (Sun) He writes nervously to George about the University Craven Scholarship, for which he is entering.

18 He sends, for George to correct, the Latin letter he must submit to his examiners.

1793

January

STC is one of the four finalists for the Craven Scholarship, but the award has to be made to the youngest of the four, Samuel Butler, later Headmaster of Shrewsbury and father of the novelist. [Butler later says that, contrary to popular accounts, STC actually worked very hard for the Craven award.] The Master of Jesus, Dr Pearce, gives STC the College 'Chapel Clerk's Place', involving £33 a year and attendance at chapel four mornings a week. STC is runner-up to John Keate in the Greek ode to astronomy submitted for the Browne Medal. His Rustat Scholarship is renewed.

February

STC writes affectionately to Mrs Evans as 'Your grateful and affectionate Boy'. He has been very ill after a tooth abscess. George informs him of Francis's death. 'He was the hero of all my little tales', says STC, but admits that 'his Death filled me rather with Melancholy than with Anguish', and that he feels very little for his brothers James and Edward.

May

William Frend is tried for sedition before the University Vice-Chancellor. (At the height of the French Revolution he had produced a pamphlet called *Peace and Union*, which created an uproar.) The undergraduates, including STC, demonstrate in his favour. STC attends the trial for eight days in the Senate House and is nearly arrested for over-enthusiastic applause. Some time this year STC reworks William Lisle Bowles's sonnet 'The River Ichen' to address the River Otter which runs through Ottery St Mary – 'Dear native brook!'.

July

STC goes to Ottery to explain his university debts to James and George. He has been 'stupified' by an enormous bill for the furnishing of his rooms, a transaction he had been duped into on his arrival at Cambridge when he had answered the upholsterer's enquiry by telling him to decorate 'Just as you please'. He also owes his tutor £50, and £8 is owed elsewhere; the total is £148. 17s. 1¼d. During this summer he flirts with Fanny Nesbitt at Exeter, takes various young ladies to the Pixies' Parlour (the small cave about a mile south of Ottery St Mary), and writes 'Song of the Pixies'. It is probably at this time that he sees his hero, William Lisle Bowles, crossing the market-place at Salisbury, but has not the courage to speak to him. At Exeter he goes to a literary society meeting where he hears a poem, 'An Evening Walk', by the young William Wordsworth, read and discussed.

September

STC lingers in London on his way back to Cambridge, to be near Mary Evans – though he dare not declare his feelings to her.

October

STC returns to Cambridge still worried by debt. [He later remembers this time as one of suicidal despair and drunkenness, but he may well be exaggerating.] His brothers have given him some money, but not enough.

November

(early) Desperately short of money, STC buys a ticket in the Irish Lottery. He sends a poem, 'To Fortune', about the event, to the *Morning Chronicle* (see below).

5   (Tues) Christopher W (WW's brother) meets STC, who talks of Bowles and of WW's own poetry, which he says is much admired in Exeter.

7   STC's poem 'To Fortune' is published in the *Morning Chronicle* and earns him a guinea. (This is his first professional publication.) CW meets STC again. More discussion of poetry.

13 First meeting of the new Literary Society in CW's rooms in Trinity. STC has not prepared the paper he had promised, but recites poetry instead.

By the middle of the month STC has fled to London, despairing over his debts and over his love for Mary Evans. He tells some Christ's Hospital boys he meets in the Angel Inn that he intends to enlist. (According to Gillman he sees a poster advertising the Dragoons and thinks: 'I've always had a violent antipathy to soldiers and horses – now's the time to get rid of it!')

December
2 (Mon) STC enlists in the King's Regiment, 15th Light Dragoons, G Troop at General Gwyn's recruiting office, Chancery Lane.
4 He accepts the 6½ guineas payment and is sworn in at Reading, where the regiment is stationed, as Silas Tomkyn Comberbache.

1794

February
Stationed at Henley-on-Thames, after two months basic training, STC is unfit to ride because of saddle-sores, and is ordered instead to nurse a fellow dragoon with smallpox. Both are isolated in the Henley pest house. The sick man survives.
6 (Thurs) STC writes angrily to fellow-undergraduate G. L. Tuckett: Tuckett has apparently divulged STC's whereabouts to his family; a letter has just arrived from his brother George which he dare not open.
8 Writes to George in hysterical apology.
20 Writes to brother James (as head of the family) for help: his discharge would cost more than 40 guineas.
23 Released from the pest house, he writes a melodramatic 'confession' to George of his misdeeds at Cambridge: 'I fled to Debauchery . . . lived in a tempest of Pleasure'.
27 George has written back and, to STC's enormous gratitude, he and brother James are taking it upon themselves to sort out his debts and negotiate his release from the army.

March
Stationed at High Wycombe, STC makes friends with the adjutant, Captain Nathaniel Ogle, who exerts himself on his behalf. Negotia-

tions continue between General Gwyn (the recruiting officer) and STC's brothers over his discharge. George in particular writes a series of personal applications to Gwyn, explaining that STC must appear in Cambridge in Easter week if he is to retain his Rustat Scholarship. (The army authorities' delay seems to be because of the difficulty of finding a substitute recruit.)

9   (Sun) George Cornish, from Ottery St Mary, makes a point of finding STC, now at Reading, whose plight has been talked of at home, and offering him money and help: he writes to his wife, 'I felt a sort of attachment for him and therefore endeavoured to find him out.'

30   STC writes to brother George about his religious faith: the beginning of his Unitarian phase.

April

4   (Fri) STC, waiting to be discharged, spends three days in Bray, near Maidenhead, 'at the House of a Gentleman [a Mr Clagget] who has behaved with particular attention to me', revising his host's work for publication and planning to write an opera with him.

7   George pays 25 guineas and STC is discharged 'insane'.

10   He returns to Cambridge, accepts a College reprimand and is gated for a month. He also has to translate 90 pages of a minor Greek writer, Demetrius Phalareus (*sic*), into English. Debts of £132.6s. 2¼d. have been paid by the brothers.

12   Official admonition by the Master of Jesus in the presence of the Fellows.

June

15   (Sun) STC sets off on a walking tour of the Wye Valley and North Wales with fellow-undergraduate, Joseph Hucks.

17?   They reach Oxford to visit STC's old friend, Robert Allen (Grecian at Christ's Hospital), who is now at University College; he takes them to meet Robert Southey at Balliol. They prolong their stay to three weeks, while STC and Southey evolve the system of Pantisocracy – an experimental society, set up after emigration to America, involving equality and self-government. Presumably it is at this time that STC meets George Burnett, RS's fellow-student at Balliol, who becomes an early recruit to Pantisocracy.

July

5   (Sat) STC and Hucks set off at last for Gloucester, ('a nothing-to-be-said-about town') and thence to Ross, Hereford, Leominster, Bishop's Castle, Welshpool, Llanfyllin, Bala, Llangollen and Wrexham.

13   STC writes earnestly to RS from Wrexham begging him not to enter the Church. (RS is at home in Bath canvassing for Pantisocrats amongst his friends.)

15   At Wrexham STC sees Mary Evans, who is visiting her grandmother. He flees without speaking to her and pours out his lovesick longings in a letter to RS. She is now engaged to another man. He writes 'The Sigh'.

21   STC and Hucks have reached Carnarvon (Caernarfon) via Ruthin, Denbigh, Holywell, Rhuddlan, Abergele, Aberconway (Conwy) and Amlwch on the Isle of Anglesey.

22   STC writes to a college friend, Henry Martin [to whom he later dedicates *The Fall of Robespierre*], that he has read a new and badly edited edition of Bowles's works; the new poems in the volume he finds 'descriptive, dignified, tender, sublime'.

28   Robespierre guillotined in France (see 22 August).

August

2   (Sat) STC leaves Hucks at Llandovery.

5   He reaches Bristol to visit Southey and Robert Lovell (RS's friend from Oxford). They develop the Pantisocratic scheme further. During the next week STC meets Joseph Cottle, a young Unitarian publisher, who offers to publish anything he writes. He also meets the Fricker family, who are bound up with the Pantisocratic project: Lovell has just married the second daughter, Mary, and RS is courting the third, Edith. By the middle of the month, apparently for the sake of Pantisocracy, STC finds himself engaged to the eldest sister, Sara.

14   STC and RS leave for Somerset to visit George Burnett at Huntspill. They walk in the Quantocks, to the Cheddar Gorge, Bridgwater and Nether Stowey, where they introduce themselves to Thomas Poole, owner of a local tannery, who is known in Bristol for his democratic views. [STC may possibly already have met him in Bristol.]

22   Back in Bristol, STC, RS and Lovell decide to raise money for Pantisocracy by writing a verse drama about the death of Robespierre. STC writes the first act, RS the second. Cottle refuses to publish. STC decides to publish it privately.

(late)   STC to London, recruiting for Pantisocracy. F. W. Franklin, a fellow-Grecian, takes him to breakfast with George Dyer, author of *Complaints of the Poor People of England* and the generation before STC at Christ's Hospital. He also visits RS's friend, Grosvenor Bedford, who sadly says he cannot join the Pantisocratic scheme.

September

In London STC enjoys preaching Pantisocracy to his old school friends Samuel Le Grice and Samuel Favell at the 'Salutation and Cat' in Newgate Street.

17   He returns to Cambridge and writes sentimentally to Edith Fricker about his dead sister, saying that he feels that he and Edith are like brother and sister.

18   He writes to RS confessing his love for Sara Fricker. (RS has encouraged this as part of the Pantisocratic scheme.)

22   *The Fall of Robespierre* published by Benjamin Flower in an edition of 500 copies. (Bowles is apparently on the list of subscribers.)

October

(early)   STC receives a letter from Mary Evans, begging him to abandon the Pantisocratic project. RS suspects him of weakening in his resolve to marry Sara Fricker; his brother George suspects him of abandoning an academic career in pursuit of a mad scheme of emigration. STC is torn by conflicting demands upon him.

21   (Tues) He sends a copy of Mary Evans's letter to RS, but insists 'I am resolved – but wretched.' Writes 'On a Discovery Made Too Late' about Mary Evans.

c.22   He is invited to spend the evening with Dr Thomas Edwards, a 'heterodox Divine' at Cambridge, and a 'Democrat' named Lushington, to talk about Pantisocracy.

November

3   (Mon) STC reads Schiller's *Robbers* and is ecstatic: 'My God! Southey! Who is this Schiller? This Convulser of the Heart?' [He later writes a sonnet 'To the Author of "The Robbers" '.] He tells RS of the death (in August) of the Reverend Fulwood Smerdon, vicar of Ottery, and sends a copy of 'Lines on a Friend' and of lines about his feeling for Mary Evans, 'When Youth his faery reign began'.

6   Writes to brother George trying to explain his political views ('Solemnly, my Brother! I tell you – I am not a Democrat').

8   To London, from where in the next few days he writes to Mary
     Evans asking if she really is engaged to Fryer Todd. She is to
     give him a definite answer about his own place in her affec-
     tions by the end of December.
Spends over a week in London following the treason trials of Hardy,
Tooke, Thelwall and Holcroft. Returns to Cambridge before the end
of the month.

December
1   (Mon) STC's series of sonnets on 'Eminent Contemporaries'
     begins to appear in the *Morning Chronicle*. It includes Joseph
     Priestley, William Godwin, Edmund Burke, William Bowles
     and RS. Eleven sonnets are printed between this date and
     29 January 1795.
9   STC is back in London. He has left Cambridge without a
     degree. Writes to RS (about his commitment to Sara Fricker),
     'My Heart is withered within me'.
9   STC's poem on Pantisocracy ('Innocent Foal! thou poor despis'd
     Forlorn!') appears in the *Morning Chronicle*. [It is later used by
     critics to satirise Pantisocracy.]
11   STC stays for a month at the 'Salutation and Cat'. Plans are
     afoot for the Pantisocratic expedition to leave for America in
     March or April 1795 – but money must be raised.
Friendship develops with Charles and Mary Lamb. (STC had known
the former slightly at school.)
24   Sends 'Religious Musings' and 'In Fancy, Well I Know' to
     Lamb. He receives a letter from Mary Evans: she is to marry
     Fryer Todd. He writes her a dignified note of farewell ('To
     love you Habit has made unalterable').
29   Writes to RS telling him of his desperate feeling for Mary and
     repeating that he does not love Sara Fricker. However he
     insists: 'Mark you, Southey! – I will do my Duty.'

1795

January
2   (Fri) STC writes to RS that he will be with him in Bristol by
     Wednesday; accordingly, RS and Lovell walk to Marlborough
     to meet the wagon – but there is no STC.

11   (Sat) Indignant at STC's failure to return to Bristol and to Sara,
      RS travels to London 'to reclaim the stray' and eventually
      tracks him down in the Unitarian Chapel with Lamb. He es-
      corts him back to Bristol.
19   STC in Bristol writes to RS in Bath, complaining of his cold-
      ness; he is also worried at RS's new idea that the Pantisocrats
      should take a Welsh farm while saving money for the trip to
      America.
By the end of the month, STC, RS and George Burnett are living
together in lodgings at 25 College Green, Bristol.
29   STC's final 'Sonnet on Eminent Contemporaries' appears in
      the *Morning Chronicle*: a savage attack on Prime Minister
      William Pitt as a 'fiend'.
(late January–early February)   STC gives three controversial 'Moral
and Political Lectures' in rooms above Bristol's Cornmarket – though
the last has to be moved to private rooms because of threatened
violence. To prove he isn't a Jacobin, STC publishes the first lecture
as a sixpenny pamphlet. [They are later published in November 1795
as *Conciones ad Populum*.] After death threats, he stops the lectures
until May.

February
(late)   He writes to George Dyer that he feels he must soon marry
Sara Fricker (whom he doesn't name): otherwise she will be driven
to marry a man she strongly dislikes. Apparently Sara, 'with her
usual Delicacy', had not told him of this possibility until he returned
to Bristol. He refers to a possible private tutoring job for the Earl of
Buchan, thanks Dyer for his help in arranging this, but says he will
have to decline the offer.

March
c.7   STC asks Joseph Cottle to lend £5 for the lodging bill. He has
       given way to RS's amended plan to establish the Pantisocratic
       community in Wales first, while saving money for the even-
       tual move to the Susquehanna in America.

April
6   (Mon) The Jesus College authorities announce that they will
     remove STC's name from the boards if he has not returned by
     14 June.

May

19 (Tues) STC begins 'Six Lectures on Revealed Religion' at the Assembly Coffeehouse on Bristol Quay, sponsored by Joseph Cottle, John Prior Estlin and the wealthy Morgan family. They also commission a portrait of STC from Peter van Dyke.

June

16 (Tues) STC's final lecture is 'On the Slave Trade' – a daring topic, as Bristol is the centre of that trade.

STC promises to stand in for one of RS's historical lectures, but fails to appear. STC, RS, Cottle, Sara and Edith Fricker go on a tour to Tintern Abbey and the Wye Valley. STC and RS quarrel.

July

RS becomes increasingly desperate to finance his marriage to Edith; disagreements with STC grow. Finally RS announces that he will rejoin Pantisocracy 'in about fourteen years'.

August

20 (Thurs) The love affair with Sara Fricker develops and STC writes 'The Eolian Harp'.

22 Though urged by his uncle, Herbert Hill, to enter the church, RS finally decides not to do so, but to study law instead.

September

1 (Tues) RS leaves College Green and returns to his mother's house in Bath.

(early) STC meets William Wordsworth for the first time at 7 Great George Street, Bristol, the home of John Pinney, a West Indian sugar merchant. WW writes 'his talent appears to me to be very great'. STC visits Stowey, and his friendship with Thomas Poole develops. He walks along the coast near Bridgwater and writes a love poem to Sara, 'Lines written at Shurton Bars'.

October

4 (Sun) STC and Sara Fricker are married at St Mary Redcliffe, Bristol, Thomas Chatterton's church. No member of the Coleridge family is present. They have a six-week honeymoon at a cottage in Church Street, Clevedon.

7 Cottle rides to pay his respects to the Coleridges and to bring a long list of domestic items STC has requested from him.

During this time STC is working on *Religious Musings* (at first called *Nativity*). He and Sara together write 'The Silver Thimble'.

November
STC returns to Bristol, leaving Sara in the cottage with her mother, her younger brother George, and George Burnett. He writes 'Reflections on having left a Place of Retirement'.

13 (Fri) Pantisocracy is finally abandoned because of RS's desertion. STC writes a long letter to RS, giving a detailed account of the progress of their friendship and accusing him of betraying his principles: 'You are lost to me because you are lost to Virtue.'

14 RS secretly marries Edith Fricker and departs for Lisbon the same day.

16 *Conciones ad Populum* is published (STC's first two lectures from the previous spring).

17 STC attends a public meeting at the Guildhall and argues in favour of a speedy ending to the war with France.

26 He delivers a lecture, 'On the Two Bills', attacking Pitt's oppressive measures to suppress sedition.

27 'On the Two Bills' is published as 'The Plot Discovered, or an Address to the People against Ministerial Treason'.

December
'An Answer to a Letter to Edward Long Fox M.D.' published. STC plans a periodical as a focus for Unitarians and moderate democrats, to be called the *Watchman*. It is to be financed by a 1000-name list of subscribers, to be collected by STC in the following months. He holds a meeting of potential Bristol subscribers, chief among whom is Josiah Wade, but doesn't invite Cottle. (He tells Cottle apologetically that this is because he has been borrowing too much money from him recently and does not want to commit him to more.)

31 (Thurs) STC attends Bristol Card Club with friends and gets drunk on 'two very small wine glasses' of punch.

1796

January
STC produces a 'flaming prospectus' for the *Watchman*. Its motto is

'That all might know the Truth and that the Truth might make us Free'.

9   (Sat) STC leaves Bristol on a five-week trip to collect subscriptions for the *Watchman*. He travels to Worcester, Birmingham, Derby, Nottingham, Sheffield and Manchester and intends to go on to Liverpool before returning to Bristol via London. He preaches in Unitarian chapels.

23?   In Derby he meets the painter Joseph Wright and the philosopher Erasmus Darwin. Argues fiercely with the latter about Revealed Religion: feels that Dr Darwin's objections are old and inadequate and not based on a fair weighing-up of the evidence.

25   In Nottingham he attends a public dinner in honour of Charles James Fox.

February

2   (Tues) STC reaches Sheffield. He is worried about the health of Mrs C, who is pregnant.

5   Reaches Manchester.

8?   Reaches Lichfield. Hears of Sara's illness. She fears a miscarriage and has moved back to her mother's house in Redcliffe. STC abandons his trip to Liverpool and hurries to be with her, having collected the 1000 subscriptions he needs.

13   Reaches Bristol.

22   Writes to Cottle that he is forced to 'write for bread' while hearing Sara's 'groans and complaints and sickness'.

In London meanwhile, Josiah Wade is drumming up support for the *Watchman*, with the help of STC's old school friend, Robert Allen.

March

1   (Tues) First issue of the *Watchman*. Nine subsequent issues appear at intervals of about eight days (to avoid the government's weekly stamp-tax). STC moves his household to Oxford Street, Kingsdown, Bristol.

9   Second issue of the *Watchman* appears. It includes an offensive text from Isaiah, 'Wherefore my Bowels shall sound like a Harp' above a satirical essay on fasts. This, says STC later, lost him '500 subscribers at one blow'.

12   STC writes to the Unitarian minister, John Edwards, that the stress of his life at the moment has obliged him to take lauda-

num almost every night. [This is the first mention of his using opium for mental as opposed to physical problems.]

19 STC thinks (wrongly) that Sara has miscarried.
20 He writes to Edwards that marriage has taught him the importance of 'that vulgar article yclept BREAD'. He has to feed a household consisting of his wife, his wife's mother and younger brother and George Burnett.
30 Poole has not received his copy of the *Watchman*. STC blames Burnett, who is in charge of distribution.

By the end of this month STC has finished *Religious Musings*.

April
16 (Sat) STC's *Poems on Various Subjects* is published by Cottle, who gives STC 30 guineas royalty. It contains 51 pieces, beginning with 'Monody on the Death of Chatterton' and ending with *Religious Musings*.

(late) STC writes admiringly to John Thelwall, imprisoned in the Tower of London for treason: 'pursuing the same ends by the same means, we ought not to be strangers to each other'. At about this time STC suffers a severe eye infection and takes laudanum 'almost every night' to soothe the pain.

May
3 (Tues) Robert Lovell dies of fever. STC has sat up all night with Lovell's wife, Mary (Mrs C's sister) and after the death he takes her and her child into his own house. Mrs C's mother is ill in his house already.
5 STC decides to close down the *Watchman*. 'O Watch Man! thou hast watched in vain', he says to Poole, quoting Ezekiel. He is £80 in debt and the periodical's moderate position is unpopular in the face of patriotic reaction to the war with France. In the letter to Poole he says that he is learning German and talks of getting a commission from Robinson 'the great London Bookseller' to stay at the University where Schiller lives, to study chemistry and anatomy.
13 In a letter to Thelwall STC refers to WW as 'a very dear friend of mine, who is in my opinion the best poet of the age'. Final issue of the *Watchman* appears. STC and Sara go away for a fortnight to stay with Tom Poole in Nether Stowey.
19 The Committee of the Royal Literary Fund for needy authors sends STC ten guineas.

31   John Fellowes, a friend made on the trip to Nottingham, has
      suggested that STC become tutor to a gentleman's family – but
      there is the problem that he is married.
Poole arranges a £40 honorarium for STC from himself, John Prior
Estlin, Josiah Wade, John Morgan and John Cruikshank. George
Dyer offers to pay off all outstanding printer's bills.

June
28   (Tues) STC addresses verses to Horne Tooke to celebrate his
      election to Parliament: 'Britons! when last ye met . . . '.

July
 1   (Fri) STC receives an offer from Perry, the editor, of the job of
      co-editor on the *Morning Chronicle* in London. (The previous
      occupant of the post, Mr Grey, has just died.) He does not like
      London, he tells Poole, but he must pursue 'those two Giants,
      Bread and Cheese'.
A rich widow, Mrs Evans, of Darley, Derbyshire, is captivated by
STC and offers him £150 a year to teach her children. STC visits
Derbyshire and leaves Mrs C there for a few days 'as my hostage'.

August
(early)   STC visits Ottery briefly, alone, and is greeted with delight
by his family.
 3   (Wed) Mrs Evans gives in to pressure from William Strutt (the
      children's legal guardian) and drops the plan to engage STC,
      though they remain on good terms and she invites him to
      return at once to Darley. She also sends Mrs C £95 for baby
      clothes.
(mid)   STC and Mrs Evans visit Matlock and Dovedale for a week.
17   Dr Crompton visits STC in Darley and offers to help him open
      a day school in Derby. STC provisionally agrees but is free to
      change his mind if something better turns up.
19   On his way home from Derby, via Burton and Lichfield, STC
      visits Thomas Hawkes in Moseley near Birmingham. He stays
      more than a week and is introduced to the young poet Charles
      Lloyd, son of a banker.

September
STC and Mrs C are together in Bristol. STC, not expecting his wife to
give birth for three more weeks, goes back to Birmingham to com-

plete plans with Charles Lloyd's father for the young man to move
in with him as a private pupil.
19   (Mon) At 2.30 am Mrs C is unexpectedly delivered of a son
     [later christened David Hartley].
20   STC receives the news and hurries home from Birmingham
     with Charles Lloyd. He is deeply moved: 'When I first saw the
     child I did not feel the thrill and overflowing of affection
     which I expected . . . But when, two hours after, I saw it at the
     bosom of its Mother . . . then I was thrilled and melted, and
     gave it the kiss of a Father' [see 1 November 1796].
22   In London, Mary Lamb stabs and kills her mother in a fit of
     insanity.
28   STC writes lovingly to Charles Lamb. [Although this is the
     only letter to survive, CL's letters show that STC wrote fre-
     quently at this time and helped CL recover from the calamity.]
(end)   RS takes the first step towards reconciliation by writing to
STC.

October
The birth of Hartley seems to have prompted STC to reject the
teaching scheme in Derbyshire and a prospect of preaching in Birmingham. Instead, he now plans to find a cottage in Nether Stowey,
to be near Tom Poole, and to bring up his children 'from their
earliest infancy in the simplicity of peasants, their food, dress and
habits completely rustic'.
(early)   STC and Charles Lloyd visit Tom Poole in Stowey.
15   (Sat) STC writes to Charles Lloyd's father outlining his new
     plans. STC edits *Sonnets by Various Authors* – which includes
     work by Lamb, Lloyd, RS and himself. 200 copies are printed
     privately.
18   He barters reluctantly with Cottle over the arrangements for
     publishing a second edition of the *Poems*.

November
1   (Tues) The first edition of STC's *Poems* is sold out. STC writes
    to Poole about his 'irrationally strong' desire to live near him.
    He encloses three sonnets written about the birth of his son.
    He prepares 'Ode to the Departing Year' for the *Cambridge
    Intelligencer*.
2   STC is struck down by a terrible neuralgic attack on the right
    side of his face. He increases the laudanum dose to 25 drops
    every five hours and sometimes raises it to 70 drops.

(second week)   Charles Lloyd has a series of fits, probably epileptic. During this time STC is writing frequently to Poole, begging him to find a cottage near Nether Stowey. He needs 'the Honey of Friendship' from Poole, he says.

19   STC includes a verbal self-portrait in a letter to Thelwall (they have not yet met): 'My face, unless when animated by immediate eloquence, expresses great Sloth, & great, indeed almost ideotic [*sic*], good nature.'

December

1   (Sun) STC writes to Poole asking him to buy on his behalf a tiny cottage in Nether Stowey at the north end of Lime Street backing on to Poole's own orchard.

(early)   Charles Lloyd returns home to Birmingham to recuperate. STC writes to Lloyd's father that he can no longer be his tutor because he now intends to devote his days to 'practical husbandry and horticulture'; Lloyd may however continue as a lodger.

12   Poole writes to dissuade STC from buying the cottage: it is too small and damp. [Perhaps he regrets committing himself to STC?]

STC writes two impassioned, grief-stricken letters in reply and Poole gives way and buys the cottage.

27   STC writes warmly to Southey, thanking him for sending a copy of his poems. (RS had taken the first step towards reconciliation in a letter to STC at the end of September.)

31   'Ode on the Departing Year' published in the *Cambridge Intelligencer*.

At the end of the month, STC, Sara and Hartley move to Nether Stowey.

1797

January

STC settles down to rural life, gardening and keeping livestock. Mrs C enjoys the company of Thomas Poole and his mother (the cottage is just behind his house and STC makes frequent use of his library). The Coleridges also make friends with John Cruikshank and his wife and baby daughter, who live nearby. He preaches at

Unitarian chapels in Bridgwater and Taunton, but otherwise does not leave home.

February
(early)   STC is commissioned by R. B. Sheridan to write a verse tragedy to be published at Drury Lane. [This he later calls *Osorio*.]
6   (Mon) STC writes the first of a series of autobiographical letters to Poole, which he 'posts' through the orchard gate dividing the two houses. These are to become the 'Biographical Supplement' to the *Biographia Literaria*. He writes an account of his idyllic life to Thelwall – 'We are very happy.'
He struggles to write a formal philosophical poem, 'The Destiny of Nations: a Vision'. This is left unfinished and eventually published in 1817 in *Sibylline Leaves*. He writes a poem too to brother George.
22   Charles Lloyd returns to live with the Coleridges.

March
5?   (Sun) STC writes the second of the autobiographical letters to Poole.
6?   Charles Lloyd begins a series of alarming fits, which last fourteen days. STC is worn out with nursing him.
10   STC sends a preface to the second edition of the *Poems* to Cottle; he is adding 40 pages of CL's poetry and 100 of Charles Lloyd's.
16   He writes to Bowles, with some poems of his own and of Lloyd's, enquiring after Bowles's mother's health.
23   STC in Bristol to visit Cottle. Borrows Brucker's *Critical History of Philosophy* from the Bristol Library. (Lloyd has gone to a sanatorium in Lichfield.)
(late)   Visits George Burnett, ill with jaundice at Huntspill.
(end March–early April)   Wordsworth calls at Nether Stowey while walking back from Bristol (where he also has seen Cottle) to Racedown in Dorset. He and Dorothy are living there at the invitation of the Pinney family. WW and STC discuss each other's work. WW meets Tom Poole, who later agrees with STC that WW is 'the greatest man he ever knew'.

April
Charles Lloyd has returned home to Birmingham, where he is put under the care of Dr Erasmus Darwin. At this stage there seems to be no ill feeling between him and STC [but see April 1798].

May

10   (Wed) STC has written 1500 lines of *Osorio*. He finds refuge from domesticity in Poole's 'book parlour'.

26   Encouraged by Poole and Cottle, STC writes a dedicatory poem for his new collection, 'To the Rev. George Coleridge', in which he explores his childhood and in which he repeatedly calls George his 'earliest Friend'. [Years later he sadly observes that despite this, George disapproved of the book.]

June

(early)   STC delivers the copy for the second edition of *Poems* to Cottle in Bristol and sets off to walk to Racedown to visit WW.

4   (Sun) He preaches at the Unitarian chapel in Bridgwater.

5   He breakfasts with Josiah Toulmin, Unitarian minister in Taunton and then sets off to walk to Racedown. He arrives at Racedown in the early evening and meets DW for the first time. Later she writes to Mary Hutchinson, who had left them the previous day, 'You had a great loss in not seeing Coleridge. He is a wonderful man. His conversation teems with soul, mind and spirit.' STC and WW read and discuss WW's 'The Ruined Cottage'. The next afternoon STC reads from *Osorio*; the following morning WW reads *The Borderers*.

10   He writes to Estlin that WW 'is a great man' and promises soon to send him a 'minute account of the bard'.

STC stays at Racedown for a fortnight.

28   WW returns with STC to Stowey. STC has invited CL, Thelwall and even RS to Stowey (perhaps with visions of a new Pantisocratic community).

July

2   (Sun) STC collects DW from Racedown and brings her to Stowey. The WWs stay a fortnight.

7   CL arrives and stays for a week. He, WW, DW and Sara walk to Alfoxden to see a waterfall. STC is left behind because Sara has accidentally scalded his foot. While they are away he writes 'This Lime Tree Bower my Prison'.

12   Poole negotiates an agreement for the WWs to rent Alfoxden House for a year. It is only four miles west of Stowey.

13   The WWs move into Alfoxden, together with Basil Montagu, son of WW's Cambridge friend, whom they are being paid to educate. STC helps them move and stays on.

17   John Thelwall arrives on a ten-day visit to Stowey. Sara takes him to Alfoxden for breakfast with the WWs and STC.

21   They all return to Stowey. Thelwall announces his desire to retire into the country. He leaves for Wales at the end of July, but asks STC to look for a house for him in the Quantocks.

(end)   Sara has an early miscarriage. Only STC knows.

August
With the threat of a French invasion in the air and the visit of the revolutionary Thelwall so recent, the WWs and STC are under suspicion. A government agent is dispatched to spy on them. He later reports to the Home Office that 'the inhabitants of Alfoxden House' are 'a Sett of Violent Democrats'. STC spreads a story that the agent, overhearing discussions of Spinoza, thought that they were referring to 'Spy Nosy'.

20   (Sun) STC exerts himself to find a house for Thelwall, writing to John Chubb, a Bridgwater magistrate. He also walks 41 miles back from Bristol, having successfully reclaimed Thelwall's lost trunk.

21   (Mon) STC sadly writes to Thelwall that even Poole is now under suspicion and that it would be better if Thelwall settled elsewhere: WW, STC and Thelwall 'separately would perhaps be tolerated – but all three together – what can it be less than plot and damned conspiracy'.

September
6   (Wed) STC sets off to visit William Lisle Bowles at Shaftesbury for a few days.

Charles Lloyd visits Stowey and Alfoxden.

10–15   Thomas Wedgwood is staying with the WWs at Alfoxden. (He is a friend of the Pinneys). STC is probably introduced to him during this time.

October
9   (Mon) STC resumes the autobiographical letters to Poole – this is the third.

He is then absent from Stowey for five days, during which time he probably goes on a solitary coastal walk to Lynton, rests at Ash Farm above Culbone Church, and writes 'Kubla Khan'. STC's note on the manuscript of the poem reads: 'composed in a sort of Reverie brought on by two grains of opium taken to check a dysentry, at a farmhouse between Porlock and Lynton, a quarter of a mile from Culbone Church, in the fall of the year, 1797.' [E. H. Coleridge places the composition a year later, because of STC's subsequent connection of the poem with the quarrel with Charles Lloyd; see May 1798 and 3 November 1810.]

14   STC finishes *Osorio*.
16   He sends a copy of *Osorio* to Sheridan at Drury Lane. The fourth autobiographical letter is sent to Poole.
28   The second edition of STC's *Poems*, with the addition of 'Poems by Charles Lamb and Charles Lloyd', is published by Cottle. Now included are 'To the River Otter' and 'Reflections on Having left a Place of Retirement'.

November

(early)   STC, WW and DW walk to Porlock, Lynmouth and the Valley of the Rocks; STC and WW plan a joint narrative poem, 'The Wanderings of Cain', for which they will write alternate stanzas. [The plan is to collapse as WW cannot sustain STC's pace of composition. STC explains much later how WW's face 'broke up in a laugh: and the Ancient Mariner was written instead'.]

13   DW reports in her letters that WW and STC conceive the 'Ancient Mariner' story during a walk over Quantoxhead to Watchet. They set out at 4 p.m. so that they can watch the sun set over Longstone Hill. WW has been reading Shelvocke's *Voyages* in which he reports the presence of albatrosses in the latitude of Cape Horn. WW soon realises that the subject is more STC's than his. [An early draft of the poem, about 300 lines, is ready by the end of November, but the completed work is not brought to Alfoxden until 23 March 1798.]

STC sends three mock sonnets to the *Monthly Magazine*, under the name of Nehemiah Higginbottom; they parody his own early poetic style and that of Lamb and Lloyd.

December

7   STC writes to Southey to deny that the second Higginbottom sonnet, 'To Simplicity', pokes fun at him. Charles Lloyd is staying with RS at the time: probably RS provides him with material to use against STC in Lloyd's novel *Edmund Oliver* (see April 1798).

STC is invited to Cote House, Westbury-on-Trym, near Bristol, home of Thomas and Josiah Wedgwood. There he meets historian James

Mackintosh, who is so impressed that he recommends STC to Daniel Stuart, editor of the *Morning Post*. Stuart invites STC to contribute regularly for a retainer of a guinea a week.

25 The Wedgwood brothers send STC a gift of £100 to support him while he writes poetry. However, that morning he also receives news that John Rowe, the Unitarian minister in Shrewsbury, is resigning his post and is to join STC's friend, John Prior Estlin, in Bristol. This opens up the possibility that STC will be offered the post. He therefore delays acknowledging the Wedgwoods' gift.

28 (morning) On the strong recommendation of Poole STC finally writes to the Wedgwoods accepting their gift, which he says will give him 'the leisure and tranquillity of independence for the next two years'. However, in the evening he receives a formal letter from Mr Isaac Wood on behalf of the Shrewsbury congregation, inviting him to become their new minister, at a salary of £120 and with a house worth £30 rent.

30 He writes to Estlin of his dilemma. He has, he says, also been considering setting up a tuition scheme with Basil Montagu, but has rejected that in favour of the ministry.

1798

January

5 (Fri) After discussions with Mrs C and Poole, STC returns the £100 to the Wedgwoods with a long covering letter explaining his financial difficulties. His annual expenditure is about £100 a year, 'including the annual £20 for which my wife's mother has a necessity'; he can earn one guinea a week writing for the *Morning Post*, but he does not approve of journalism as a lifetime's career. He feels the need for a secure income for his family and he must therefore accept the post in the Unitarian ministry.

6 He is now 'utterly without money' and has to borrow from Estlin and Wade.

8 'Fire, Famine and Slaughter' published in the *Morning Post*.

14 STC preaches a sermon in the Unitarian chapel at Shrewsbury, which is a great success. Meets William Hazlitt (aged 17), the son of the Unitarian minister at Wem in Shropshire.

15   STC stays overnight with the Hazlitts. Next morning he receives a letter from the Wedgwoods offering him £150 a year for life to devote himself to poetry and philosophy. William Hazlitt witnesses the moment when he decides to accept, 'in the act of trying on one of his shoes'. He accompanies STC for six miles on his way back to Shrewsbury and is invited to visit Stowey in the spring.

17   STC writes to accept the Wedgwoods' offer. He writes to Poole, 'I am not certain I am not dreaming.'

30   He returns to Bristol and spends a week at Cote House with the Wedgwoods.

February
Some time this month STC writes 'Frost at Midnight'.

9   (Thurs) STC returns to Stowey.

11   Walks with DW near Stowey. [DW records the following months in detail in the *Alfoxden Journal*, but often makes errors over dates: she talks of 'walking with Coleridge' on 3, 4 and 5 February, when in fact he was still in Bristol with the Wedgwoods.]

12   Walks with DW back to Alfoxden.

13   Walks with DW through the wood.

17   STC and WW walk to visit WW's landlord, Mr Bartholemew. STC writes to Cottle: he is considering including 'The Ancient Mariner' and *Osorio* in the third edition of his poems.

19   The fifth and last of the autobiographical letters to Poole.

21   STC calls at Alfoxden.

22   STC calls at Alfoxden in the morning and stays for dinner.

23   STC and WW walk together (morning).

26   STC and Mr and Mrs John Cruikshank of Nether Stowey call (morning) at Alfoxden. WW and DW walk back most of the way with STC after dinner.

27   DW visits Stowey (evening). STC returns with her in bright moonlight as far as the wood.

March
2   (Fri) STC at Alfoxden. DW walks part of the way home with him.

6   DW visits Stowey (evening). Finds STC 'very ill'. The WWs are to leave Alfoxden at midsummer; it has been let to the Cruikshanks.

7 STC (ill with an abscessed tooth) writes to Cottle about Charles Lloyd. Angry at being parodied in the Higginbottom sonnets, Lloyd has asked Cottle to remove his poems from the proposed reissue of the *Poems* of STC, CL and Lloyd. He and CL plan their own joint venture. [This appears during 1798 as *Blank Verse By Charles Lamb and Charles Lloyd*.] STC is hurt and says that he is glad to have Lloyd's poems removed from his collection. He writes too about plans for a third edition of his own *Poems*, 'a volume worthy of me', in about ten weeks time. [This never materialises.] WW and DW have tea at Stowey. They see a solitary leaf whirling in the wind at the top of a tree (see 'Christabel', i. 49–52).

8 STC to Alfoxden after dinner. 'The Old Man of the Alps' published in the *Morning Post* under the pseudonym 'Nicias Erythraeus' (see also 13 April).

9 STC and Mrs C to Alfoxden for ten days. DW walks out to meet them. They discuss plans for a trip to Germany.

10 STC writes a conciliatory letter to brother George about his future plans: he is not a radical in politics any longer – 'I am of no party'; he is to devote himself to poetry. 'I love fields and woods and mountains with almost visionary fondness.' STC and the WWs walk in the evening to the top of the hill.

12 Tom Poole to supper at Alfoxden (and on the next day.)

13 STC writes to Cottle on behalf of WW: what would Cottle offer to publish (a) *Osorio* and *The Borderers*, and (b) 'Salisbury Plain' and 'The Ruined Cottage'? He and WW need the money for the German tour and are therefore planning a joint enterprise. [This eventually emerges as the *Lyrical Ballads*.]

16 WW, DW and STC go for a short walk in the park. WW unwell, but better by evening and they walk to Putsham.

c.17 STC writes to Cottle that he will not attend Dr Thomas Beddoes's Chemical Lectures in Bristol in the next few weeks, much as he would like to, as Mrs C is 'within a month of her time'. He himself is well: '[M]y new & tender health is all over me like a voluptuous feeling.'

18 STC and Mrs C return to Stowey. The WWs walk halfway home with them.

20 STC dines at Alfoxden.

21 The WWs to Stowey for tea.

23 STC walks to Alfoxden for dinner, bringing with him the completed ballad, 'The Rime of the Ancyent Marinere'.

24 STC, the Chesters and Ellen Cruikshank all to Alfoxden.
25 The WWs to Stowey for tea. They do not reach home until 1 a.m.
26 Tom Wedgwood stays at Stowey. The WWs visit him there.
29 STC to Alfoxden for dinner.

April

During this spring and summer STC is working on 'Christabel', 'The Dark Ladie', 'The Three Graves', 'Fears in Solitude' (written as a French invasion is expected), 'The Nightingale' (probably written at Alfoxden at the end of this month) and 'Recantation: an Ode'.

(early) STC writes to Cottle that he and WW have decided not to publish their Tragedies after all. They will find the money for the German expedition some other way.

2 (Mon) STC to Alfoxden to escape the smoke in his cottage (there is a high wind). He stays overnight.
3 STC, WW and DW walk to Crowcombe (possibly to appeal to a friend of the owner of Alfoxden for an extension of the lease).
5 STC to Alfoxden for dinner.
6 DW walks part of the way home with STC (morning).
c.10–18 STC goes to visit his brother George and his mother at Ottery.
13 The WWs have supper at Stowey. 'Lewti' published in the *Morning Post* under the pseudonym 'Nicias Erythraeus' (see 8 March).
16 'France: An Ode' published in the *Morning Post*.
18 STC dines with the WWs and they walk him home.
24 STC again at Alfoxden. The WWs walk him home.
25 STC drinks tea at Alfoxden. The WWs walk him home.
26 STC drinks tea with DW while WW goes to have his portrait painted by W. Shuter.

Charles Lloyd's novel *Edmund Oliver* is published during the month and upsets STC so much that he is distracted from his work. (See letter to CL in May; in a Notebook entry for 3 November 1810, he says that it was this quarrel which prevented him from finishing 'Christabel').

May

(early) STC writes to CL in sadness at Charles's involvement with Lloyd. (Edmund Oliver is dedicated to CL.) He blames Lloyd rather than CL: 'From you I have received little pain.' He cannot believe that 'Edmund Oliver's love-fit, debaucheries, leaving college and going into the army' have no connection with himself. [CL and STC remain estranged until 1800, but thereafter their friendship is to be unbroken.]

7   (Mon) STC to Alfoxden. DW walks back with him to Stowey.
8   STC dines at Alfoxden.
9   WW has received Charles Lloyd's works from Cottle, but has not yet read Edmund Oliver.
10 STC sends WW a copy of his poem 'The Nightingale'.
13 He takes the service for Dr Toulmin at Taunton and walks home.
14 Berkeley Coleridge born at 1.30 a.m.
16 STC, WW and DW set off to visit the Cheddar Gorge and stay overnight at Bridgwater.
17 They tour the Gorge and caves and stay overnight at Cross, near Axbridge.
18 WW goes on to Bristol, hoping to see Charles Lloyd at Southey's and effect a reconciliation with STC. Lloyd, however, has left for his father's home in Birmingham.
20? William Hazlitt visits Stowey and is brought to Alfoxden, where he reads the manuscript for *Lyrical Ballads* and stays overnight. On the following morning STC reads 'The Idiot Boy' aloud in the park. The next day they spend at Stowey, the next at Alfoxden.
(late) Cottle comes to Stowey and Alfoxden to discuss plans to publish the *Lyrical Ballads*. They all walk to Lynmouth and back. The day after Cottle's departure, STC walks to Linton, stays overnight and returns the next day. He writes to Cottle that he has decided not to dedicate the *Lyrical Ballads* to the Wedgwoods: he will wait four or five years until he has something substantial to offer them.

June
11 (Mon) Hazlitt's three-week visit ends. He and STC travel to Bristol.
12 STC spends the day with Estlin, who violently opposes the German expedition.
13 To Brentford near London, where he stays with Poole's friend, Samuel Purkiss.
14 Purkiss drives STC most of the way to Josiah Wedgwood's new house at Stoke, near Cobham in Surrey.
18 DW writes to her aunt that she and WW intend to stay cheaply

in Germany for at least a year and that they expect the Coleridge family to go with them.

25 The WWs leave Alfoxden for Bristol, staying for a week with the Coleridges on the way. The St Aubin family have refused to renew their lease after June because of local suspicions about their 'spying' activities.

Lloyd writes to Cottle this month, 'I love Coleridge, and can forget all that has happened.'

July
2 (Mon) The WWs and STC set off for Bristol. The WWs go on to tour the Wye Valley and visit Tintern Abbey.

August
3 (Fri) STC writes to Poole from Bristol that he will not take his family to Germany after all, for reasons of expense. He intends to stay abroad for three or four months. The visit, he says, is 'of high importance to my intellectual utility; and of course to my moral happiness'.

4? STC persuades WW and DW to 'dart into Wales' with him to visit John Thelwall for a week on his farm at Llyswen on the Wye near Brecon.

September
(early) The *Lyrical Ballads* is published anonymously. It contains 19 poems by WW and four by STC: the 'Ancient Mariner', 'The Nightingale' and two extracts from *Osorio*, 'The Foster-mother's Tale' and 'The Dungeon'. STC, in London on his way to Germany, meets Mrs Barbauld. He also introduces himself to Joseph Johnson the bookseller, of St Paul's Churchyard, quickly makes friends with him and arranges that Johnson will publish 'Fears in Solitude', 'France: an Ode' and 'Frost at Midnight'. [This small quarto volume comes out during this year and sells no more than 200 copies.]

14 (Fri) STC, WW, DW and John Chester (a Stowey farmer friend) leave London for Yarmouth.

15 They reach Yarmouth at noon. STC has some long conversations with George Burnett there.

16 They sail for Hamburg at 11 a.m. STC is very conscious that this is his first trip abroad. As the land disappears, he has a vision of his children.

18 STC writes lovingly to Mrs C from the ship moored 30 miles from Cuxhaven: 'Over what place does the Moon hang to your eye, my dearest Sara? To me it hangs over the left bank of the Elbe.' *Lyrical Ballads* published.

19 Arrival at Hamburg.

20 They meet the younger brother of the German poet, Klopstock. In the evening they see an 'execrable' French comedy.

21 STC and WW are taken by Victor Klopstock to visit his brother Friedrich, the poet. He and WW talk in French for an hour about poetry, but STC in his notebook finds him 'disappointing'. News reaches England of Nelson's victory at the Battle of the Nile (1 August).

22 They talk of moving on either to Weimar or to a village near Hamburg. The Weimar journey is considered dangerous.

23 (Sun) DW too unwell to visit churches with the others. STC is shocked to find shops open for half the day: 'I'm a strict Sabbatarian myself.' STC and Chester set off for Ratzeburg (35 miles from Hamburg) by stage coach.

24 They reach Ratzeburg and find it 'neat and pretty'.

25 When STC arrives at a concert, the band strikes up 'Rule Britannia' in honour of Nelson's victory. STC stays up until 4 a.m. and writes 200 lines of verse.

26 STC arranges lodgings for Chester and himself with Pastor Unruhe in Ratzeburg. They eat at the table d'hôte in honour of Nelson.

27 They return to Hamburg via Empfelde.

28 They are reunited with the WWs, who are looking for cheaper lodgings.

29 Feast of St Michael, patron saint of Hamburg, but it is, says STC, 'all as quiet as a Bristol Sunday!'

30 STC and Chester leave for their new lodgings in Ratzeburg at 7 a.m.

October

3 (Wed) The WWs leave Hamburg for Goslar in Upper Saxony. WW wants seclusion to work. He does not write to STC for six weeks, which the latter finds 'ominous'.

11 STC by boat to Lübeck on the Baltic and thence to Kiel.

16 To Travemunde.

20 He writes to Mrs C of his comfortable life at Ratzeburg. He has

translated one of his poems, ' "Charles! my slow heart was only sad when first" ', into German, to the admiration of his new friends.

During the autumn STC works intensively on the German language and German literature. He works through Karl Wilhelm Ramler's verse translations of Horace's *Odes* and of Catullus; he reads Luther's letters; he transcribes a newspaper article on the suicides which were linked with the publication of Goethe's *Sorrows of Young Werther* in 1774; and he plans a life of Gotthold Ephraim Lessing, based on the brief account by Johann Friedrich Schink.

November

26 (Mon) STC pines for letters from England. He writes to Mrs C that there is snow and hard frost; he is learning to skate. Ladies try to persuade him to dance, but he is not in dancing mood.

31 He at last receives a letter from Mrs C: 'God be praised that my Babes are alive.'

December

(early)   A letter arrives from Mrs C (dated 1 November) saying that Berkeley has been seriously ill after a smallpox inoculation.

(mid)   STC sends to the WWs in Goslar some emotional 'English hexameters' beginning: 'William, my head and my heart! . . . Dorothy, eager of soul, my most affectionate sister!' and ending 'but I am lonely and want you!'

31 Mrs C takes Berkeley, who is now consumptive, to her mother's house in Bristol.

1799

January

4 (Fri) Having been cut off from news of England during the winter (post has been held up because the Elbe is frozen), STC at last receives a letter from Poole. He replies at once: he is extending his stay from three months to eight and hopes to enrol in the University of Göttingen until the end of the academic year, which means that he will back in Stowey in May. He reveals that he and the WWs have been discussing by letter

where they should settle in England. WW is drawn back to the North, but says he cannot be without STC.

February

6 (Wed) STC leaves Ratzeburg on a six-day journey via Hanover to Göttingen.

11 Berkeley Coleridge dies of convulsions in Bristol. Mrs C is taken in and cared for by the Southeys in Westbury. Poole persuades her to keep the news from STC because it would disrupt his German studies.

12 STC reaches Göttingen and enrols at the University.

March

Continued absence of letters from England because of the frozen Elbe. In England Mrs C writes to Poole that the *Lyrical Ballads* 'are laughed at and disliked by all with very few exceptions'. STC is enjoying academic life. He has made friends with a group of English students, Charles and Frederick Parry and Anthony Hamilton, all of Cambridge, and Clement Carlyon and George Greenough. He works at the second part of 'Christabel'.

25 (Mon) STC reports, 'Chester and STC in a damned dirty hole in the Burg Strasse in Göttingen', short of cash!

April

4 (Thurs) STC hears at last of Berkeley's death in a letter from Poole dated 15 March.

6 STC writes to Mrs C, sending an epitaph for Berkeley; he mentions their marital differences (for the first time) and hopes the death will bring them together – yet he insists on continuing his German studies 'for ten or twelve weeks more'.

18? A letter arrives from Mrs C, broken-hearted at the loss of Berkeley. STC is shaken but still determined to stay.

20 or 21 The WWs visit STC in Göttingen. They are eager to return home and urge STC to return with them. They are disappointed that he will not consider leaving Poole in Stowey: they want to settle again in the Lake District and hope that he will move to be near them.

23 STC replies to Mrs C: he must stay longer to finish the book on Lessing and save the family from debt. He sends her the poem later published as 'Something Childish'.

May

6 (Mon) STC sends Poole an adaptation of a poem by Samuel Gottlieb Burde, 'Das Heimweh in August 1780'. He speaks of his own intense homesickness.

11 STC sets off on an expedition to the Brocken in the Hartz Mountains, hoping to see the famous spectre. With him go Chester, the Parry brothers, Greenough, Carlyon and the son of Professor Blumenbach of the University. They dine the first day at Hessa Drensch, five miles from Göttingen; the countryside reminds STC of Stowey. They visit Womarhausen, 'the first Catholic village I have seen'. Thence to Schlachtfeld, 'an ugly Hanoverian village'.

12 (Whitsun eve) To Andreasburg.

13 They reach Raschenbach, 'the roaring brook', then Elbingerode.

14 They leave Elbingerode for Rubeland and stay at Blankenberg where 'we heard much of the French king'.

15 To Osterode, then Catlenberg.

16–17 After dining at Wernigerode they find they still have fifteen miles to walk to reach Goslar (where the WWs had stayed). STC writes to Mrs C and sends her a copy of the poem, 'I stood on Brocken's sovran height'.

18 Back to Göttingen.

21 He writes to Josiah Wedgwood that he has 'six huge Letters' waiting for him, which he had planned to send with Hamilton. However, Hamilton's departure has been delayed. STC is unwilling to risk the letters and now plans to bring them home himself. He tells of the background work he has done for the Life of Lessing. He has also bought £30-worth of books, mostly metaphysics, for the 'one work, to which I hope to dedicate in silence the prime of my life'.

June

STC sends to the Wedgwoods, with Anthony Hamilton, a specially commissioned pastel portrait of himself by a local Göttingen artist.

23 (Sun) Professor Blumenbach gives a huge farewell party for STC and Chester.

24 They set off for home, via the Brocken again, accompanied by Greenough and Carlyon. They leave Göttingen at midday, travel by coach to Möllnfelde, dine at Northeim and arrive at Clausthal at 11.30 p.m. They approach the Brocken, but still fail to see the spectre.

27 They reach Blankenburg by a different route from last time.
30 They reach Brunswick and meet the Parry brothers.

July
3 (Wed) The party splits up. Chester and STC leave the others at Brunswick and go on to Wolfenbuttel, where STC tries unsuccessfully to obtain material on Lessing. They then walk to Helmstedt, where they see the priceless sketches by Holbein, Raphael and Caravaggio.
18 They reach Cuxhaven. STC has lost some chests of books. [These do eventually reach him in England.]
28? STC arrives in Stowey (having probably visited Daniel Stuart of the *Morning Post* in London on the way).
29 At Mrs C's insistence STC writes to Southey asking for a reconciliation, after all his kindness to Sara at the time of Berkeley's death.

August
(early) Mrs C and Hartley to Minehead, to holiday with the Southeys.
8 (Thurs) STC writes a second letter to RS, explaining Charles Lloyd's mischief-making.
(mid) The Southeys come to Stowey, bringing home Mrs C and Hartley. STC and RS embrace in Lime Street when they meet. The two families spend the rest of the summer together, househunting for RS in Somerset, visiting Ottery, touring Devon via Dartmouth and Totnes.

September
(early) STC spends some time with Josiah Wedgwood at Upcott in Devonshire. He is trying to regain Alfoxden for the WWs to keep them in the south.
6 'The Devil's Thoughts', a joint production of STC and RS, is published in the *Morning Post*.
10 The Southeys are now in lodgings in Exeter; STC and family are with them. STC and RS are planning a brief walking tour together.
10? STC has heard from WW who seems unhappy: STC suspects Basil Montagu of cheating him financially. He writes to urge WW to work steadily at 'The Recluse' and to write a blank verse poem for those in despair over the failure of the French Revolution.

13 Hartley falls downstairs at RS's lodgings in Exeter and sprains his arm.

16 STC and RS return from their walking tour.

24 The Coleridge family return home. Hartley has caught scabies: the cottage at Stowey has to be fumigated and H painted with brimstone ointment. Sara shows 'hypersuperlative Grief', writes STC unsympathetically. STC and RS are working at an ambitious poem in hexameters on Mohamet. [Only 14 lines by STC and 109 lines by RS are ever written.]

(end) The cottage is flooded in the seasonal rains.

October

12 (Sat) STC writes in delight to thank WW for addressing 'The Recluse' to him.

(early) STC has spent a few days with the Wedgwoods at Upcott.

16 or 17 STC to Bristol. His friendship with Humphrey Davy develops. He plans to go on to London to look for his missing chests of books. [These in fact arrive in Stowey two days after his departure.]

22 Instead of going to London, STC travels north with Cottle to visit the WWs. He has heard worrying rumours about WW's health [but that could be his excuse for changing his plans; Mrs C thinks he is still in Bristol and does not hear from him again until December].

26 STC and Cottle reach Sockburn Farm in County Durham, where the WWs are visiting their childhood friends, the Hutchinsons. This is his first meeting with Sara Hutchinson. His *Notebook* records for this day, 'Few moments in life so interesting as those of an affectionate reception from those who have heard of you yet are strangers to your person.'

27 STC, WW and Cottle set off for the Lake District.

30 Cottle leaves them at Greta Bridge to return to London. STC and WW go on by coach to Temple Sowerby, where they are joined by WW's younger brother, John.

31 All three visit a relative of WW's at Barton, then stay the night at Bampton.

November

1 (Fri) STC, WW and John W walk to Kentmere by Haweswater and Long Sleddale.

2 To Windermere (Bowness); then over the lake to Hawkshead.

3   Round Windermere to Rydal and Grasmere.
5   They climb Helvellyn. When they reach Grisedale Tarn, John
    W leaves them to go on to Ullswater and Newbiggin.
8   They leave lodgings in Grasmere for Keswick and stay near
    Bassenthwaite at Ouse Bridge.
10 They reach Keswick. STC receives a letter from Daniel Stuart
    offering him a contract as a staff writer on the *Morning Post.*
    He writes to RS saying that he plans to accept.
11 Having visited Cockermouth and explored Keswick, they go
    to Lorton, Crummock Water and Buttermere.
12 They climb Scale Force into Ennerdale.
14 They go on from Wastdale to Borrowdale.
15 They visit the Lodore Falls, the Druids' Circle and Threlkeld
    below Saddleback.
16 To Matterdale, Aira Force and Ullswater.
17 They visit Thomas Clarkson (campaigner against the slave
    trade) at Eusemere.
18 STC leaves WW but, instead of going to London, he goes back
    to Sockburn, where he stays a week and falls in love with Sara
    Hutchinson.
24 He records an episode in his *Notebook* (in Latin) in which he
    held Sara's hand behind his back for a long while and 'then for
    the first time, Love pierced me with his dart, envenomed and
    alas! incurable.' STC writes to RS that he has bought a copy of
    'The Beauties of the AntiJacobin' (in which his character is
    vilified as one who has left his native country and 'left his poor
    children fatherless and destitute'). He is wondering whether
    to prosecute the publishers for libel.
26 He catches the all-night coach to London to take up the job on
    the *Morning Post.*
27 He reaches London and lodges at 21 Buckingham Street, The
    Strand. He writes for his wife and Hartley to join him.

December
Some time early in this month Mrs C and Hartley arrive from Stowey.
DW and WW move to Town End in Grasmere (later Dove Cottage).

7   (Sat) STC's first regular piece appears in the *Morning Post*:
    an analysis of the new French Constitution proposed by
    Napoleon.
12 A leading article by STC proposes a new realism. He is now
    more sober and less radical.

20 WW and DW move to Dove Cottage.
21 STC's poem, 'Love', inspired by Sara Hutchinson, appears in the *Morning Post*. (In this early version it is called the 'Introduction to the Tale of the Dark Ladie'.)
24 He writes to report his progress to RS: he says he is 'a pure Scribbler'. He plans to pay off the £150 overdrawn on the Wedgwood annuity by April 1800, by which time he will have finished the Lessing biography. [It never appears].
25 'A Christmas Carol' published in the *Morning Post*. The Coleridge family dine with William Godwin. Hartley is criticised by Godwin for his 'boisterousness'. In contrast, STC finds Godwin's children's 'cadaverous silence' 'quite catacombish'. [Their behaviour is probably linked to the recent tragic death of Mary Wollstonecroft.]
28 STC and RS plan negotiations with Thomas Longman, the publisher. STC sends RS his poem, 'A Christmas Carol'.

1800

January
1 (Wed) STC, writing to Humphrey Davy, dreams of 'a little colony' consisting of Davy, Tobin. WW, RS and himself. He realises that this is 'the precious Stuff For Dreams'.
(early) Writes to Tom Wedgwood of his frequent contact with Godwin, whom he likes because he thinks so well of Davy. To STC, Davy is an extraordinary young man, but there is one even more remarkable human being in his life (obviously WW). He writes articles for the *Morning Post* in the afternoons and evenings and fills the mornings with literary work. 'I work from I-rise to I-set', he tells Poole. He writes mainly on foreign policy: though he thinks Bonaparte's method of gaining power wrong, he attacks Pitt's government for not accepting Napoleon's offer of peace negotiations. Between December and April he writes about 40 articles. He visits the theatre frequently and is introduced at last to Sheridan, whom he dislikes. Develops a friendship with Perdita Robinson, the Shakespearian actress.
22 (Wed) Attends the first of James Mackintosh's lectures on 'The Laws of Nature and of Nations'. (These continue until 6 February.) STC dislikes Mackintosh's ideas. He writes to

Poole, who is helping him find a new house in Stowey, mentioning directly the incompatibility between himself and Sara.

February

4 (Tues) Reports Pitt's speech of 3 February. During this month he reports three all-night sittings of the House of Commons and finds it 'too, too fatiguing'.

10 Attends and makes notes on Sheridan's speech in the House of Commons for the *Morning Post* of 11 February.

17 Reports Pitt's speech in the House explaining that the war with France must go on for reasons of national security. This is published in the *Morning Post* on 18 February and much praised.

18 Declares (in a letter to Southey), 'I shall do no more for Stuart' – but in fact goes on for several more weeks.

During this month STC is translating Schiller in 'very polished blank Verse'. He has made the acquaintance of Thomas Longman, the publisher.

March

1 (Sat) Tells Stuart he is busy translating Schiller's three *Wallenstein* plays for Longman: he will go on working for Stuart, 'but not for any regular Stipend – that harrasses me'.

2 Mrs C and Hartley leave London to spend a month with the Roskillys at Kempsford. STC moves in with the Lambs at 36 Chapel Street, Pentonville.

15 He tells Samuel Purkiss that he plans to publish an account of his tour in the north of England: Longman will advance him £100 immediately. [Neither the advance nor the book materialises.]

19 STC's 3000-word profile of Pitt appears in the *Morning Post* – his masterpiece.

21 He writes wistfully to Poole of WW that 'the Society of such a Being is of priceless Value' but that 'he will never quit the North of England'.

STC dines during this month with Lamb, Godwin and various 'literary ladies', including Miss Mary Hays, Miss Benger, Mrs Barbauld, Miss Charlotte Smith and Miss Sarah Wesley. The *Notebooks* record that he has found a lock of Sara H's hair in his pocket. [Cf. 'The Keepsake', published in the *Morning Post*, 17 September 1802, but, says STC, 'composed two years before'].

31 STC replies to a letter from Poole which charges him with 'prostration in regard to WW'. He suggests that he is merely recognising genuine greatness – 'Is it impossible that a greater poet than any since Milton may appear in our days?'

April

2   (Wed) Lamb reports that 'C has left us on a visit to his God, Wordsworth.'

6   STC reaches Grasmere and stays exactly four weeks (his first visit to Dove Cottage). During this time he discovers that Greta Hall, Keswick, is to let. He and WW plan to prepare a two-volume edition of the *Lyrical Ballads*, the second consisting of new poems. Although STC has pressing obligations of his own – including the Life of Lessing promised to the Wedgwoods – he throws himself wholeheartedly into WW's schemes, which include making large-scale revisions to the 'Ancient Mariner'. (WW thinks this poem discouraged readers of the first edition by its strangeness.)

10 RS and Edith are leaving for Portugal. STC writes to him that 'if you stay longer than a year on the Continent, I and mine will join you'.

20 The first part of *Wallenstein*, STC's translation of Schiller, is finished.

May

4   (Sun) STC sets off for Bristol, taking copies of poems for the *Lyrical Ballads*. He arranges for the work to be printed by Biggs and Cottle and proofread by Humphrey Davy, then chemist at the Pneumatic Institute, Clifton. Longman is to be the publisher.

21 STC, staying at Poole's, writes to Godwin that, if he cannot find a suitable house in Stowey, 'I return to Cumberland and settle in Keswick.'

June

12 (Thurs) STC writes to Josiah Wedgwood from Bristol, returning his £20 advance; his househunting in the Stowey area has been in vain, so 'I shall move Northward'. STC believes that Poole will go abroad once his mother dies and seems resigned to the need to move to be near WW. DW is negotiating on his

behalf for Greta Hall, Keswick, with the owner, William Jackson.

13 The Coleridge family begin a leisurely journey north, sleeping at Tewkesbury, Shrewsbury and Chester and then staying for over a week with the Crompton family outside Liverpool.

29 STC, Mrs C and Hartley arrive at Dove Cottage, where they stay until 23 July. DW records many details of daily life there in the *Grasmere Journals* (until January 1803). STC is ill with rheumatism, but he and DW prepare copies of poems for the new *Lyrical Ballads*.

July

STC's *Notebooks* record encounters with country people; he also climbs Dungeon Gill Force in Langdale.

20 (Sun) STC meets Mr and Mrs Sympson at Grasmere.

23 The WWs and STC and family picnic on an island on Grasmere Lake.

24 STC, Sara and Hartley move into Greta Hall, Keswick. The owner, Mr William Jackson, lives in rooms at the back of the house with his housekeeper, Mrs Wilson, who is to become a favourite with Hartley. STC writes at once to Josiah Wedgwood, confessing his grief at parting from Poole: 'For him & for myself in him I should have given Stowey a decisive preference.' He lists, however, the arguments against Stowey: there was no suitable house; Mrs C had no friends there; the nearness to Bristol brought him into too close contact with Mrs C's family; Poole's relations have been rude to them; and in any case, Poole is determined to go abroad when his mother dies. (He never mentions WW. The Wedgwoods have been very much against the move nearer WW: Tom Wedgwood apparently has made a doomladen prophecy about WW which only STC has seen.)

In the first few days after his arrival, STC writes ecstatic letters from the rooftop of Greta Hall, to Davy, Tobin and Purkiss.

31 STC to Grasmere until 2 August, copying poems for the *Lyrical Ballads*.

August

1 (Fri) STC and WW walk to Ullswater and on their return read WW's poems.

2 STC and WW to Keswick (WW stays four days).
6 STC writes to Sara H that he has climbed Sca Fell with only a walking stick to help him.
8 WW and DW to Keswick, where they stay a week, during which time STC goes to church. [Is this rare?]
9 He walks with DW in the Windy Brow woods.
11 He and DW walk to Windy Brow.
16 STC walks with DW, intending to pick raspberries.
24 He walks to Latrigg with Mrs C and Hartley.
27 He climbs Skiddaw for the first time, an event recorded in 'A Stranger Minstrel', dedicated to the actress Perdita Robinson.
29 He walks to Grasmere over the Eastern Fells and climbs Helvellyn by moonlight.
31 He walks to Grasmere over Helvellyn and reads part of 'Christabel' to the WWs.

During this month and the next STC writes 'A Thought suggested by a View of Saddleback in Cumbria', 'The Mad Monk', 'Inscription for a Seat by the Roadside' and 'A Stranger Minstrel'.

September
1 (Mon) WW reads 'To Joanna' and 'The Fir Grove' to STC. They bathe in a stream. After dinner STC discovers a rock seat in the orchard and clears away the brambles from it. He has to go to bed after tea. DW brings him a broiled mutton chop, which he eats in bed. STC and DW talk until nearly midnight.
3 STC, WW and John W climb Helvellyn with Mr Sympson; STC returns to Keswick.
14 10.30 p.m. Birth of Derwent Coleridge. STC at first wants to call him 'Bracy', after the minstrel in 'Christabel'.
16 STC writes to Godwin asking to borrow £10 (he cannot, he says, ask Poole or the Wedgwoods, as they were all so strongly against him moving north). [He repays this debt to Godwin promptly].
23 STC to Grasmere.
26 He returns to Keswick with Robert Jones, WW's old college friend.
27 Derwent, sickly and not expected to live, is baptised.
28 STC writes to Stuart of the many articles he is preparing for the *Morning Post*.
30 He sits up all night 'writing essays for the newspaper', says DW. Derwent has been ill with convulsions. STC writes of his concern for WW's health.

October

4 (Sat) STC to Grasmere, afraid for WW's health. He reads the second part of 'Christabel' to the WWs for inclusion in the *Lyrical Ballads*. WW and DW 'exceedingly delighted' with it.

5 STC reads 'Christabel' again; 'we had increasing pleasure', writes DW. STC 'intending to go but did not get off', says DW. They walk after dinner to Rydal.

6 WW decides after all not to include 'Christabel' in *LB*: it will be discordant with his own poetry. He plans to publish it with his poem 'The Pedlar' instead. [This never happens.]

7 STC leaves for Keswick at 11 a.m.

11 He climbs Carrock Fell in dangerous weather and 'almost broke my neck'.

13 He admits to Godwin that the effort to finish 'Christabel' for inclusion in the *Lyrical Ballads* has put him far behind in his money-earning activities.

22 STC to Grasmere. DW comments in her *Journal* that he 'had done nothing' (that is, on *LB*). After supper WW reads 'Ruth' and STC 'Christabel'.

23 STC returns to Keswick with John Stoddart.

Charles Lloyd and his wife and child have moved to Brathay near Ambleside – 'an unwelcome addition', says DW. STC claims he is indifferent: 'I have no wish to see him and I have no wish not to see him.'

November

1 (Sat) STC writes to Josiah Wedgwood, volunteering to be Tom's companion on any future journey abroad for his health. (Tom has just returned from the West Indies, where at least he grew no worse.) He talks with thinly disguised pain of WW's rejection of 'Christabel' and of his own increasing problems with procrastination; he admits to missing Tom Poole and Stowey. He apologises for overdrawing £40 on the annuity for 1801.

(early) STC's eyes are badly inflamed.

14 The WWs receive two letters from STC who is 'very ill'.

15 WW after tea to visit STC because of his illness.

16 STC writes that he is better.

18 STC and WW to Penrith to meet Sara H, who is coming to spend the winter at Grasmere.

28 STC walks to Grasmere. He is ill, with boils on his neck. He suffers a terrible nightmare. WW cries out aloud in the night on hearing STC scream.

December

2   (Tues) STC returns home in rainy weather.

4   He goes back to Grasmere. He eats nothing, says DW, 'to cure his boils'.

5   STC and WW set off to Keswick, but are 'forced to turn back' because the wind is bad for STC's eyes.

6   STC home to Keswick. He writes to Poole that he had meditated on calling Derwent 'Thomas Poole Coleridge' but had decided against it, as it might not have pleased Poole's family. He speaks of his determination to write more: in the last year 'I have too much trifled with my reputation.'

10   The WWs to Keswick until 14 December. They find STC better.

15   STC writes to Longman that the *Lyrical Ballads* has been completed and posted. He writes again about the proposed publication of the account of the German tour: 'your Printer shall not have to complain of an hour's delay'. [However, he sends nothing further and the project is dropped.]

17   He writes consolingly to Godwin on the poor reception of his first play.

18   'Michael' is sent to the printers. Lines 1–206 are copied by STC, the rest probably by Sara H. Mrs C and Derwent to Grasmere.

20   STC to Grasmere, where he falls ill with rheumatism.

25   For Christmas STC gives Sara H a copy of Anna Seward's *Original Sonnets*; he inscribes them 'to Asahara, the Moorish Maid' – an early version of 'Asra'. Sara H copies five pages of native plant names into STC's *Notebook*.

During this month STC finishes editing the *Lyrical Ballads* for WW. He plans to visit Poole in Stowey, but is prevented by ill health.

1801

January

STC is ill and confined to bed with rheumatism during the first three months of the year. He experiments with ever-higher doses of opium to combat the pain.

7   (Tues) He writes to Poole of his money worries – he is in debt to WW, to various shopkeepers in Keswick, to CL and to Poole himself.

25? (Sun) *Lyrical Ballads* (second edition) published under WW's
name but acknowledging five pieces by 'A Friend'. These are
the original four and 'Love' (a longer version of which had
been published in the *Morning Post*, 21 December 1799 as
'Introduction to the Tale of the Dark Ladie'). The 'Ancient
Mariner' has been removed from the front of Volume I to the
back.

February
STC embarks on a study of philosophy, beginning with Locke
and Descartes. He writes a series of letters on the subject to Josiah
Wedgwood.

3 (Tues) STC writes to Humphrey Davy of William Calvert's
idea to move with the WWs into Windy Brow, only half a mile
from Greta Hall. Calvert wants to study chemistry with STC
and WW.
(mid) Sara H goes to Keswick to help the Coleridges.
(late) WW reports in a letter to Francis Wrangham, vicar of
Hunmanby, that STC is 'very unwell' and is thinking of going abroad
to improve his health.

March
16 (Mon) STC writes excitedly to Poole of his philosophical
progress: 'If I do not greatly delude myself, I have not only
completely extricated the notions of Time, and Space; but have
overthrown the doctrine of Association, as taught by Hartley.'
WW is worried at the effect of too much thought on STC's
health; STC has therefore undertaken to take a week off to
prepare 'Christabel' for publication, 'in order to get rid of all
my engagements with Longman'.
(late) WW and Sara H visit STC. STC talks eagerly to Sara and
reads from Bartram's *Travels*; later this month she returns home to
Sockburn.
25 STC writes to Godwin that, with so much philosophising, 'the
Poet is dead in me'.
27 WW makes himself responsible for repayment of the £30
Longman has advanced to STC for the Life of Lessing.

April
13 (Mon) STC writes to RS, describing Greta Hall: 'The house is

twice as large as we want . . . I know no place in which you and Edith would find yourselves so well suited.'

18 He writes to Poole in despair at the state of the country.
19 WW and DW to Keswick to help nurse STC.
23 STC writes to Thelwall 'that (at all events, if I stay in this climate) I am going down into the Grave'.
29 DW writes to Mary Hutchinson that Mrs C is an 'excellent nurse' to her children, but is incompatible with STC because of her lack of 'sensibility'.

May

STC continues to write gloomy letters to Davy, RS and the rest about his health.

6 (Wed) He includes in a letter to RS a poem about Hartley: 'A little child, a limber Elf' – which is later printed in 1816 as the conclusion to Part II of 'Christabel'.
7 (Thurs) STC to Grasmere with Hartley. He stays eight days, then leaves Hartley behind with DW for a while.
17 In a letter to Poole STC refers casually to his use of 'Brandy and Laudanum' during his illness. [This supports his later assertion that he fell into drug addiction unwittingly, simply as a means of relieving pain.]

STC begins Hartley's formal education, at Mrs C's request: they explore natural history together.

June

18 (Thurs) STC climbs Easedale, finds a long, narrow hollow and tries symbolically burying himself.
23 A change in the weather makes STC bedridden once more.

During this month the poet Samuel Rogers is brought to the Lake District by Richard Sharp to meet WW and STC.

July

5 (Sun) STC sends £10 to Mrs Fricker in Bristol. He speaks in a letter to Poole of spending winter in the Azores for his health.

(early) WW writes to Thomas Poole to see if he can raise money to send STC abroad. £50 would be enough to send him to the Azores. Poole writes back directly to STC to say he can only manage £20. However, an unexpected £50 arrives from Josiah Wedgwood.

16 STC to Durham to read Duns Scotus in the Cathedral Library.

He meets Sara H at her brother George's new farm at Bishop's Middleham, eight miles from Durham.

25 He writes from Durham to RS, suggesting that they and WW go to live on St Nevis in the West Indies, on Pinney's estate: 'I feel, that there is no relief for me in any part of England. – Very hot weather brings me about in an instant – & I relapse as soon as it coldens.'

(late) STC rides back with Sara H to her brother Tom's farm, 60 miles away, at Gallow Hill near Scarborough, for sea-bathing. (His knee has swollen up with gout.)

31 They reach Gallow Hill. STC stays for ten days.

August

9 (Sun) STC leaves Gallow Hill and returns to Bishop's Middleham and thence to Dimsdale in Staffordshire for a week's sulphur baths.

15 He sends 'On Revisiting the Seashore' to RS (published in the *Morning Post*, 15 September).

24 His books are returned to Durham Cathedral Library.

25 STC back in Keswick for a visit from RS and his family.

STC this month contributes five poems to the *Morning Post*.

September

RS and family are still with the Coleridges.

7 (Mon) STC writes scathingly of his Ottery family to Poole – 'I do not love them – their ways are not my ways . . . I have no recollection of childhood connected with them, none but painful thoughts . . . '.

19 He writes affectionately and tearfully to Poole on the death of Poole's mother: 'She was the only Being whom I ever felt in the relation of Mother.'

22 He writes to Godwin that he has had to give up the idea of going to the Azores because of lack of money, but that he must not spend another winter in the 'wet and cold' of the Lake District.

October

10 (Sat) STC at Grasmere; builds 'Sara's Seat' with the WWs on Dunmail Rise [later referred to in 'Dejection: an Ode']. STC then leaves for Keswick.

15   He visits the Luffs at Ambleside and finds the WWs there.
21   He writes to RS (who is about to depart for Dublin as Secretary to the Irish Chancellor) that Mrs C and he are 'not suited to each other' but that 'I have thought through the subject of marriage and am convinced of its indissolubleness.'

November

(early)   STC supervises Hartley's 'shortening' – moving from baby clothes to boy's trousers. 'If my wife loved me, and I my wife, half as well as we both love our children, I should be the happiest man alive – but this is not – will not be!' he writes to RS.
 6   (Fri) STC to Grasmere.
 9   WW, DW and Mary H to Keswick with STC. Mrs C and the children are at Eusemere with the Clarksons. DW comments pointedly on how comfortable they all were at Keswick (by implication, because of Mrs C's absence).
10   The WWs leave for Grasmere and STC sets off to London for the winter, stopping first at the Clarksons to say goodbye to his family. DW has wept at his departure. In letters she refers to 'poor C.' and writes, 'O! how many reasons have I to be anxious for him – .'
16   STC in London, at first at RS's lodgings, 25 Bridge Street, Westminster.
*c.*25   He moves to 10 King Street, between Covent Garden and Fleet Street. His landlord is Howell the tailor and the lodgings were found for him by Stuart. He plunges into newspaper work. Sees much of Godwin, Lamb, Davy and so on.

December

 7   (Mon) WW, DW and Mary H visit Keswick and see Derwent, 'pale, the image of his father' and are charmed by Hartley.
13   DW writes in her journal that she has had a letter from Sara H: 'Sara in bad spirits about C.'
21   WW writes to STC, hearing he has been ill again 'in his bowels'. 'We were made very unhappy', writes DW in her *Journal*.
25   STC has Christmas Day breakfast with Humphrey Davy.
26   To Poole at Stowey. Stays three weeks but refuses to visit Ottery.

1802

January
21 (Thurs) STC back in London, attends Davy's lecture at the Royal Institute – He writes to congratulate Godwin on his marriage: 'I wish you all happiness & moral progression.'
22 He writes revealingly to Godwin, 'I am a starling self-encaged and my whole Note is, Tomorrow and Tomorrow and Tomorrow.'
29 The WWs receive 'a heart-rending letter' from STC; WW talks of going to London to see him.

February
STC composes newspaper articles furiously. Writes to his wife: 'I am now quite a man of fashion'; talks of plans for the whole family to live abroad for two years. Tells Poole that he now has 'no need of opiates'.
29 Having heard that Sara H is ill, STC leaves London for the north.

March
2 (Tues) STC reaches Gallow Hill, stays ten days helping Tom and Mary nurse Sara. (He has not told the WWs of his visit.)
13 STC leaves Gallow Hill. He records that he 'wept aloud' as the coach pulled out.
15 STC reaches Keswick. There is a reconciliation with his wife.
19 STC to Grasmere. DW 'agitated very much': STC seems 'half-stupified' (opium?). They talk of WW's forthcoming marriage to Mary H.
21 STC back to Keswick.
28 WW and DW to Keswick till 5 April. WW reads stanzas of the Immortality Ode to STC. [Echoes of it occur in 'Dejection: an Ode' – see 4 April.]
29 STC with WW to Armathwaite.

April
1 (Thurs) STC, WW, DW and Sara C walk to the How; home via Portinscale.
3 STC and WW climb Skiddaw.
4 STC begins a verse letter to Sara H and continues it far into the

stormy night. ['Letter to Sara Hutchinson' is eventually published, much altered, as 'Dejection: an Ode'.]

5   The WWs leave Keswick for the Clarksons at Eusemere. STC walks with them as far as Threlkeld.
20 STC to Grasmere after tea.
21 He reads 'Letter to Sara' to the WWs. DW is 'in miserable spirits'.
22 They walk to Easedale. STC talks of his plan of sowing laburnum in the woods.
23 They walk towards Rydale and to Nab Scar. STC finds them 'a Bower' to rest in.
24 They walk to Rydale. STC stops up a rivulet to make a lake.

May

During this month STC and Mrs C quarrel fiercely, but then find a new peace together which STC hopes 'will be permanent'.

4   (Tues) STC meets the WWs at 'Sara's Crag'. He goes on writing to Sara H during the summer – 'my darling Sara'.
12 STC to Grasmere. Talks late into the night with DW.
13 STC back to Keswick despite snow showers.
15 The WWs receive a melancholy letter from STC and WW resolves to go to Keswick next day.
17 DW to Keswick till 19.
19 STC sets DW home at half-past nine in the morning.
20 The WWs receive a letter from STC saying that he wishes them not to go to Keswick (presumably because of Mrs C's jealousy?).
22 STC meets the WWs at 'Sara's Rock': 'We had some interesting melancholy talk about his private affairs', says DW in her *Journal*.

June

3   (Thurs) STC sends a friendly letter to his brother George via the Reverend R. H. Froude, visiting the WWs from Devon.
10 STC reaches Grasmere 'with a sackful of books etc. and a branch of mountain ash. He had been attacked by a cow. He came over by Grisedale', writes DW.
12 He returns home.
22 The second edition of the *Lyrical Ballads*, with an extended Preface, arrives at Grasmere.
23 STC reaches Grasmere and stays until 30 June.

July
9 (Fri) STC walks to meet the WWs, who stay in Keswick for a few days.

12 STC walks six or seven miles with the WWs towards Eusemere, where they are to stay overnight on their way to France: they are going to settle affairs with Annette Vallon before WW's marriage to Mary H.

(mid) STC makes a new friend of William Sotheby, poet and dramatist, to whom he writes six long letters on Romantic criticism between July and September.

19 He includes in a letter to Sotheby a reworked version of the 'Letter to Sara' with 'William' taking the place of 'Sara'.

27 STC writes a long and cheerful letter to Sara H recounting Hartley's exploits. [This, and another dated 10 August 1802, are the only complete letters to have survived.]

29 He writes to RS about WW's new Preface to the *Lyrical Ballads* and about his differences with WW over poetry; he also talks of a 'happy Revolution' in his marriage; and he works hard to persuade the Southey family to share Greta Hall with him.

August
1 (Sun) STC sets off on a solitary walking tour of the Lakes, during which he writes ecstatically to Sara H. He walks through Newlands to Ennerdale, where he stays the night with John Ponsonby, a friend of his landlord, Mr Jackson.

2 After spending most of the day with Ponsonby, he sets off after tea and walks to Egremont, then on to St Bee's where, since he cannot get a bed, he sleeps at a pothouse.

3 Returns to Egremont, visits the castle, sleeps there.

4 Walks to Calder Abbey, to Wastdale, to Keppel Crag and Kirkfell, where he stays the night with Thomas Tyson (he had slept there with WW nearly three years before.)

5 He climbs Scafell and pours forth an extempore poem [which later shrinks to become 'Chamouny', a translation and adaptation (unacknowledged) from the work of the German poetess, Friederika Brun]. (See 11 September.)

6 To Devock Lake, sleeps at Ulpha Kirk.

7 Through Donnerdale Mountains to Broughton Vale and on to Coniston.

8 Explores Coniston, on to Brathay; sleeps at Charles Lloyd's house near Ambleside.

9   To Grasmere and back to Keswick.

(mid)   Charles and Mary Lamb arrive, unannounced, at Keswick and stay for three weeks. During the visit STC and CL walk to Moss Force and STC writes a vivid description.

September

During this month STC writes frequently for the *Morning Post* – four long articles on the French Republic and a series of disguised 'Asra' poems about his love for Sara H.

2   (Tues) STC writes to RS with detailed plans for him to move into Greta Hall with his family, to live with the Coleridges.

6   'The Picture' published in the *Morning Post*.

9   STC writes 'To Mathilda Betham from a Stranger' and sends it to Miss Betham.

11   'Chamouny: the Hour before Sunrise' published in the *Morning Post*.

(mid)   He visits Brayton Hall to use Sir Wilfred Lawson's 'kingly library'. Visitors to Greta Hall this month include Sir Charles and Lady Boughton with Miss Boughton, Miles Peter Andrews and Captain Topham – 'We have been plagued to death with a swarm of visitors', says STC.

October

4   (Mon) WW and Mary H are married at Brompton Church in London. 'Dejection: an Ode' appears in the *Morning Post*.

11   STC to Grasmere. Stays till 13.

12   Walks with the WWs to Rydale.

13   STC, WW, Mary W and DW all to Keswick. DW writes: 'We consented, Mrs C. not being at home.'

17   'The Keepsake' published in the *Morning Post* (written Spring 1800).

19   'The Daydream: from an Emigrant to his Absent Wife' published in the *Morning Post*. [Another linked but much more personal poem, 'A Daydream', which talks of 'Mary' and 'Asra', was probably written at the same time – though not published until 1828.]

During this month and November, STC publishes open letters in the *Morning Post* to Charles James Fox, challenging his view of Bonaparte as a peacemaker. STC now sounds not radical but conservative.

November

4 (Thurs) STC sets off suddenly for the West Country to join Thomas Wedgwood who is mortally ill and in need of a travelling companion on a journey to recuperate in France. Mrs C, who is expecting a baby in January, is furious at the idea of STC going to France.

5 Because of a missed coach connection, STC can spend a day in Penrith with Sara H, who is staying with relatives there. Mrs C hears of this and angry letters are exchanged during November and December. STC gradually wins her over again.

8 STC arrives in London.

(mid) He joins Tom Wedgwood at Cote House.

13 They travel into Wales, to Usk and then to Abergavenny and Brecon, on their way to visit some Wedgwood cousins in Pembrokeshire.

20 At St Clear's, Carmarthen.

21 They reach Cresselly and stay at the home of Mr Allen, father of the Mrs Wedgwoods. STC flirts with the cousins, Jessica, Emma and Frances. He writes to his wife, analysing both their characters at length and concluding that 'in sex, acquirements, and in the quantity and quality of natural endowments whether of feeling or of Intellect, you are the inferior'. He suggests that Sara H should nurse Mrs C during her lying-in – so that his wife 'should get to know her better'. He also encloses a £50 advance on the Wedgwood annuity.

December

5 (Sun) STC writes one of several affectionate letters to his wife, discussing possible names for the baby about to be born ('Algretha, Rotha, Laura, Emily . . . The Boy must be either Bracey or Crescelly [sic]').

Between October and December STC has been writing to the *Morning Post* about the Maid of Buttermere – turning himself into a popular journalist. Sara H comes to stay at Grasmere over Christmas and is ill with toothache. Tom Wedgwood is too ill to travel abroad, so he and STC set off to the Lakes.

16 STC writes 'with trembling' to his wife, hoping she is safely delivered by the time she reads his words; he warns her that Tom Wedgwood will be returning with him, but only for a day or two – 'do not let him be any weight or bustle on your mind – let him be entirely Mr Jackson's visitor.'

21 STC's seminal article on Jacobinism in England appears in the
    Morning Post.
23 (Thurs) Sara Coleridge born prematurely at 6 a.m.
24 STC and Tom Wedgwood reach Grasmere. On hearing of his
    daughter's birth, STC takes TW immediately to Keswick.
30 DW to Keswick to help Mrs C and the baby. STC takes TW to
    see Captain Charles Luff at Patterdale: he is to be TW's sport-
    ing companion.
31 STC returns to Grasmere over the Kirkstone Pass.

1803

January
2   (Sun) STC, WW, Mary W and Sara H walk halfway to Keswick
    to meet DW on her way home from helping Mrs C.
5   STC writes to his wife from Grasmere of the need for her to
    like Sara H. He hints at a secret of Sara H's which he cannot
    put in a letter. [This could be the possibility of her marrying
    John W.]
6   STC revisits Captain Luff at Patterdale, gets soaked in a storm
    and returns to Grasmere.
7   He rides with Sara H 'on a double horse' to Keswick, where
    she stays a few days. During the stay they walk together to
    Lodore at the far end of Derwentwater.
8   He writes to praise RS for his kind treatment of George Burnett:
    'For myself, I have no heart to spare for a Coxcomb mad with
    vanity and stupified with opium.'
20 STC leaves home to join Tom Wedgwood in Bristol.

February
STC spends the month like 'a Comet tied to a Comet's tail', with Tom
Wedgwood, planning a trip through France and Italy to Sicily; he
travels between Cote House, RS's lodgings in Bristol and Poole at
Stowey. He writes to Samuel Purkiss asking him to procure some
Indian hemp from Sir Joseph Banks, to help relieve Tom's 'hopeless
malady'. [This is described as 'thickening of the gut' – probably
stomach cancer – and is the disease from which he will soon die.]
17 (Thurs) STC writes to RS about the plan for the Southey fam-
    ily to move into Greta Hall: he encourages him to 'emancipate

yourself' from the widowed Mrs Lovell (née Mary Fricker), who has been living with them. Mrs C will not have her sharing the house too.

24 STC at Josiah Wedgwood's house, Gunville, Blandford, Dorset, where he tries the hemp on TW. It does not help.

March

STC in London during this month, seeing, among others, John Rickman. He applies for life insurance for his family so that he can go abroad.

14 (Mon) STC makes a will naming Poole and the WWs as first and second trustees for his family. He arranges with Longman for a third edition of the poems, but leaves Lamb to do the editing.

24 Mary Lamb has one of her fits while STC is in the house. He takes her in a hackney coach to the madhouse in Hoxton, trying to soothe the distraught Charles.

In London STC sees Davy, Sotheby and Sir George Beaumont, a wealthy art patron who at first dislikes him.

April

7 (Thurs) The official commencement of the life insurance policy, which would bring Mrs C £1000 in the event of STC's death. [The premium is high – £27 per annum – but STC keeps it up for the rest of his life.]

8 He returns to Keswick, the probability of war with France ending plans to travel to the Continent. He is ill in bed with rheumatic fever for a month.

28 Sara H leaves Grasmere to return home.

May

All the Coleridge family fall ill with influenza, but all survive.

June

Longman and Rees issue a third edition of the *Poems*. CL has seen it through the press. STC writes frequently to Godwin and Southey with grand plans for a book – 'an Instrument of Practical Reasoning', a 'curious metaphysical work' which, he says, has been in his mind since December 1801. Nothing comes of this book and this summer is generally unproductive.

18 (Sat) John W is born prematurely.

July
Hazlitt and the Beaumonts visit STC during this month.
17   (Sun) John W's christening. STC is a godfather. Richard
      Wordsworth and DW are the other godparents.
STC writes articles for the *Morning Post* supporting the government
in their stand against France. (War has been renewed over the sover-
eignty of Malta.) STC is now openly against Fox.

August
 9   (Tues) Samuel Rogers and his sister have tea at Grasmere and
      meet WW and STC. [STC writes later, contemptuously, of 'the
      crazy Hovel of that poor Man's Heart'.]
12   WW and DW travel to Keswick in their new jaunting car. STC
      tells them of Sir George Beaumont's generous offer: he will
      build WW a new house at Applethwaite, three miles from
      Greta Hall, so that he can be near STC. STC begins to plan a
      trip to Malta, where there is a British naval base and where
      he could get an administrative post under his acquaintance,
      John Stoddart, newly appointed Judge Advocate there.
13   STC sends to the Beaumonts a copy of WW's 'Resolution and
      Independence' and of his own 'Dejection: an Ode'. (This con-
      firms the close link between the two poems.)
14   WW and DW again to Keswick.
15   They set off in the jaunting car with STC for a tour of Scotland.
      Spend the night at Hesket Newmarket.
16   STC meets the confidence trickster, John Hatfield, the seducer
      of Mary Robinson, in the gaoler's house in Carlisle. (See De-
      cember 1802 and 'The Maid of Buttermere' in *The Prelude*.)
      [Hatfield is executed later this month.] They sleep at Longtown
      at the 'Graham's Arms'.
17   They cross into Scotland and reach Dumfries.
18   To Burns's grave. STC unwell in the evening.
19   They stay at the village of Hopetoun.
20   To Lanark and the Falls of Clyde.
21   Sleep at Hamilton.
22   Reach Glasgow, after visiting the castle at Bothwell.
23   To Dumbarton.
24   To Loch Lomond, staying overnight at Luss.
25   Mrs C writes charitably of STC to RS: 'My husband is a good
      man . . . I should be a very, very happy Woman if it were not
      for a few things – and my husband's ill health stands at the
      head of these evils!'

26 By boat to Rob Roy's cave, then to Inversnaid.
27 WW and DW across to Rob Roy's grave by ferryboat; it is too cold for STC who walks instead and meets them later. To the ferryman's cottage for the night.
29 STC decides to send his clothes to Edinburgh and make his way there on foot. He leaves the WWs just beyond Arrochar.
30 He changes his mind and turns north, walking via Glencoe and Ballachulish towards Fort William. He intends to follow the line of forts to Inverness.

September
5 (Mon) To Fort Augustus, where he is arrested as a spy, but soon released. On by Inverness to Cullen.
10 Reaches Perth, where a letter awaits him from Southey. RS's only daughter, Margaret, has died and he and Mrs Southey, with the widowed Mrs Lovell whom STC detests, have all fled to Greta Hall. [They are to stay there for the rest of their lives.] STC writes at once to RS, enclosing 'The Pains of Sleep'.
STC takes a coach to Edinburgh, where he is delayed for two or three days waiting for another coach. During this time he climbs Arthur's Seat at sunset.
15 He reaches Keswick.

October
STC and RS take many walks over the fells. STC is in frequent touch by letter with Sara H. Thomas Clarkson visits him.
3 (Mon) STC writes to Poole of the terrible nightmares which afflict him. He screams so much that he is 'a Nuisance in my own House'.
9 WW calls on STC after his return from Scotland. Joanna Hutchinson is staying at Grasmere – very ill and upset because her brother Tom has received notice to quit Gallow Hill. WW has ridden to Keswick in search of medical advice for her.
14 WW writes belatedly to Sir George Beaumont to thank him for his gift of land at Applethwaite (so that WW may be near STC). He says he is unlikely to build a house there, as STC is intending to live abroad for his health. STC writes to Poole criticising WW: 'I now see very little of WW . . . [he is] living wholly among Devotees.'
c.24 Hazlitt returns to Keswick to finish portraits of STC and Hartley.

26 WW and Hazlitt upset STC by being irreverent: WW criticises Paley, Ray and Derham.

November

13 (Sun) DW writes to Catherine Clarkson that Tom Hutchinson has taken Park House Farm near Eusemere: she therefore hopes that STC and Sara H will be neighbours next summer.

All the Coleridge children are baptised (David Hartley is now simply Hartley). During this month Hazlitt is forced to flee from the Lake District after a mob pursue him because of his indecent assaults on women. He is hidden, first at Greta Hall and then at Grasmere. WW gives him money and clothes for the journey. He leaves his sketches behind. [STC writes to his wife the following March that, if she has no wish for 'that rude sketch of my Face up in the upper book room Garret', then perhaps Sara H might like it.]

25 STC writes to Thelwall (about to visit him from Kendal) asking him to bring 'an Ounce of crude opium and 9 ounces of Laudanum', packed up to withstand a long journey. He plans to go either to Malta or Madeira for his health, the war with France having closed all other routes.

December

5 (Mon) STC writes to Matthew Coates for an introduction to a relative of his wife's on Madeira, Dr Joseph Adams, whose pamphlet on Madeira he has just read. [It is Adams who in 1816 recommends STC to James Gillman.]

20 STC is at Grasmere with Derwent for DW's birthday on Christmas Day. He had intended to go abroad at once, but is taken ill and nursed by DW, who is shocked by his regular screaming and nightmares.

31 WW and STC walk up Greenhead Gill to the sheepfold, where WW reads 'Michael'.

1804

January

4 (Wed) STC still convalescing at Grasmere, preparatory to going abroad. High above Grasmere, WW reads to him 'the second part of his divine Self-Biography' (*The Prelude*). WW

begs STC to map out for him a plan for the philosophic poem, 'The Recluse', which he is to write while STC is abroad. WW arranges a loan of £100 for STC via Sir William Sotheby.

14 STC suddenly recovers his health and (accompanied by WW as far as Troutbeck), he walks 19 miles to Kendal, in 4 hours and 35 minutes, without being fatigued.

16 He spends a week in Liverpool with Dr Crompton.

23 He reaches London and joins Poole, who is there to work with John Rickman on the Census. Poole allows STC to work in his own lodgings at 16 Abingdon Street, Westminster. STC sleeps at Waghorn's Coffeehouse nearby. He contributes six pieces for Stuart's new evening paper, the *Courier*, and agrees to go on writing for Stuart while abroad, on British foreign policy.

29 After hearing from Humphrey Davy a 'spirited Eulogy' of a tour with Greenhough to Sicily, he decides to go there, via Malta.

31 He breakfasts with Richard Sharp MP.

February

2 (Thurs) STC dines with the Godwins at the Lambs and has a dreadful quarrel with Godwin's second wife, for which he apologises profusely the next day, blaming 'a large glass of Punch before supper' and the fact that he is very sensitive about his religious opinions.

7 STC visits Sir George Beaumont at Dunmow; he invites himself for two days, but stays for ten, during which time he has a fall from a horse. He also meets Joseph Farington, the diarist, who later records his impressions.

8 He writes to WW of how blessed WW is, because his 'Path of Duty lies through vine-trellised Elm-groves, through love and joy and grandeur'. WW is working, at STC's suggestion, on his 'Ode to Duty'. (In December, STC had written of the need for duty and inclination to coincide.)

14 He writes to Mrs C that she must draw money while he is away from an account left with Daniel Stuart. He speaks gratefully of RS's 'Vice-fathership' of his children.

17 Sir George presses £100 into STC's hand as he leaves Dunmow.

18 Back in London, he borrows rooms from his old friend, James Tobin, at 17 Barnard's Inn, Holborn.

19 STC writes to Mrs C that Hartley must go to the Town School, if a 'steady lad' can be found to take care of him there. He

writes at length about the children: he is sending the boys a game of Spillikins.

March

During his time in London, waiting to procure a passage on a ship, STC meets Sheridan, Campbell, Sotheby, Richard Sharp, Grosvenor Bedford and Greenhough. He writes letters of farewell to RS, WW and Tom Wedgwood (who is preparing for death.) James Northcote paints his portrait.

10 (Sat) STC dines at CL's. He sends to Sara H a volume of Sir Thomas Browne's Works, which CL has managed to find for him. It contains *Pseudoxia Epidemica, Religio Medici, Hydriotaphia* (a meditation on burial urns) and *The Garden of Cyprus.*

(mid) Sir George Beaumont comes to London and invites STC to his house in Grosvenor Square for the remainder of his time in England.

12 WW stands security for the repayment of £100 to Sotheby, who gives STC a cheque for that amount for his journey. STC books his passage to Malta on the *Speedwell*, Commander: John Findlay, for 35 guineas. He visits John Rickman, Secretary to the Speaker of the House of Commons, and both try to help the ill-fated George Burnett, who is by now stupified with opium addiction.

DW and Mary W have made a 'complete copy' of WW's poems to be STC's 'companions in Italy'; they amount to about 8000 lines. STC's plan is to stay in Sicily at the Benedictine convent, with the help of Lord Nelson and Lady Hamilton. He will go first to Malta, where he has letters of introduction from Sotheby to Sir Alexander Ball, the High Commissioner, and General Villettes, the military commander.

27 He hurries to Portsmouth at the order of the captain of the *Speedwell*, as a convoy has been arranged. He is weak and ill.

28–30 He stays at the Crown Inn, Portsmouth, expecting to depart any day.

April

1 (Sun) He moves to lodgings at Mr J. C. Motley's in Thomas Street, from where he writes with great affection to Mrs C.

6 Even on the eve of departure, STC is trying to find a job for Mrs C's brother, George. He boards the *Speedwell* and writes farewell notes to Lamb and Stuart (who had both seen him off

in London), and to WW, RS, Rickman and Beaumont.

9 The *Speedwell* sails.

20 They reach Gibraltar, where the *Maidstone* takes over the convoy.

21 STC writes an account of the journey to Daniel Stuart.

25 They leave Gibraltar and suffer 24 days of storm and dead calms until they reach Valletta.

The *Notebook* entries speak constantly of STC's anguished love for Sara H.

May

18 (Fri) STC arrives, unexpected, at John Stoddart's house in Malta.

19 He walks around the harbour with the Stoddarts.

20 To church; calls on the High Commissioner, Sir Alexander Ball.

21 Sir Alexander Ball visits STC. In a thunderstorm STC has trouble with his breathing.

22 Rides to Saint Antonio, visits St John's.

23 Calls on General Villettes.

Sir Alexander Ball takes him up and gives him comfortable quarters in the palaces of Valletta and San Antonio; he is employed in secretarial work at £25 a month.

June

13 (Wed) The WWs visit Greta Hall and see the Coleridge children – Hartley almost 8, Derwent nearly 4, Sara 18 months, delicate, 'like a fairy'.

July

4 (Wed) STC invited to the palace by Ball for breakfast; nearly faints on seeing someone who reminds him of Sara H.

6 Writes to Stuart, 'now I know that a change of climate and an absence from (England) and inward Distractions were necessary for me. After being near death, I hope I shall return in Spirit a regenerated Creature.'

7? STC moves to the palace and daily contact with Ball. [He later refers to it in *The Friend* as 'the most memorable and instructive period of my life'.] He takes the place of one of Ball's three secretaries, E. T. Chapman (away in Odessa), as a writer of memoranda.

11 STC transfers to San Antonio at a time of very hot weather.
13 Writes his third political paper for Ball, about Malta's retention and importance, with a view to publishing it in England. (He hopes to clear the £100 loan from Sotheby.) During this time he writes 'The Blossoming of the Solitary Date-tree' and refers often in his *Notebooks* to Sara H. He begins the promised letter to WW on 'The Recluse'.
16 He records a few earthquake shocks.
25 The first convoy from England since his arrival: STC hopes in vain for news of his children. On this day at Grasmere the Coleridge children are staying with the WWs. There has been no news from STC since his departure. STC meets Major Adye on the newly-arrived convoy and arranges to travel to Sicily and Syracuse with him and return to Malta for the winter.

August
9 (Thurs) STC receives £50 from Macaulay, the elderly Public Secretary, as two months' salary for his work in Chapman's absence; Ball orders that he should be kept on the payroll.
10 STC crosses to Syracuse, with a letter of introduction to G. F. Leckie, the English consul. He spends the first week in quarantine, then goes to Catania.
19 Travels on to Etna.
Stays till *c*.26 and ascends Etna twice, but probably (because of absence of specific references in the *Notebooks*) not as far as the crater.
27 STC back in Syracuse at Leckie's estate on the site of Timoleon's Villa.
29 Mrs C at last receives a letter from STC: he has been very ill on the journey.

September
27 (Thurs) The opera season opens in Syracuse. STC becomes absorbed and writes at length in his *Notebook* about music and harmony. He flirts with the prima donna, Cecilia Bertozzoli. [Later he says that it was the 'heavenly vision' of Sara H's face which rescued him from succumbing to her charms.]
This month the WWs decide to remain in Dove Cottage, despite its inconveniences, until they know where STC will settle on his return. They realise that he cannot live in the north again because of his health.

October

10 (Wed) STC still in Syracuse, writing another political paper.

19 RS writes to STC that Mr Jackson, the landlord, has sold Greta Hall and that Mrs C has been given notice to quit by Whitsuntide; Southey says that Mrs C will move into furnished lodgings until STC's return.

21 On his birthday STC chides himself in his *Notebooks* over his lack of effort as a writer and his habit of 'bedrugging the feelings'. [He has noted the extensive cultivation of narcotics in Sicily, but it is not clear if he himself has used them here.]

November

6 (Tues) STC exchanges legal arguments with the governor over the capture and ransom of two English merchant vessels. He then returns hastily to Malta to explain what has happened to Ball.

8 STC, back in Malta, is put in quarantine. (Rigid precautions are being enforced to prevent the spread of the yellow fever epidemic in Gibraltar.) Ball asks STC to undertake the dangerous commission of taking over £70,000 to buy corn in Odessa; STC at first refuses, then, 'in a fit of despair, when life was a burthen to me', he accepts – but has to wait for Captain W. M. Leake to take him, and meanwhile stays in Malta as undersecretary. [The project later falls through, but not before it has caused great anxiety in Grasmere and Keswick.] STC's rooms have been given to someone else in his absence; he has to transfer to the Treasury across the street, where he stays until his departure from Malta.

23 Another convoy arrives from England – but still no letters from home for STC. [He does, however, probably receive a copy of the *Courier*, as he copies out in his *Notebook* an article about the great storm in East Anglia and the Midlands of 13 August 1804.]

STC enjoys riding with Ball around the island; he calls it 'heavenly' and his health is 'greatly improved'. Yet in his *Notebooks* he still pines for Sara H – 'oh Sara! I am never happy, never deeply gladdened.'

December

7 (Fri) STC finishes a corrected version of his *Observations on Egypt*, written earlier for Ball.

12 Spain declares war on England. STC writes to Mrs C: should he remain in Malta hoping for preferment from Ball and a post in Sardinia, or return to England in the New Year? The real issue is that of the breakdown of the marriage: 'O God! O God! if that, Sara! which we both know too well were not unalterably my lot, how gladly would I prefer the mere necessaries of life in England . . . '. He is reading avidly, particularly Kant and Herman Reimarus.

23 He falls into 'involuntary intoxication' after drinking to cure colic pains and writes a drunken letter to Southey about his unhappy marriage. At home, the WWs and Mrs C are 'exceedingly anxious' at not having heard from him yet.

Over Christmas STC writes many letters home and sends them off in two separate packages.

1805

January

5 (Sat) DW writes to Lady Beaumont that the sale of Greta Hall has fallen through; Mrs C and the Southeys may therefore stay as tenants. They still have no news of STC.

11 A convoy is moored off Valletta, anticipating storms; in impatience STC sends out a small boat to collect letters and at last receives one from WW, one from Mrs C and one or more from Sara H. Sara's letters seem to express lack of hope and STC himself is 'fearfully despondent'. He hears of the death from plague in Gibraltar of Major Adye, to whom he had entrusted a batch of letters and papers. These have now been burnt as plague-papers.

18 Alexander Macaulay, the old Public Secretary, dies and STC is appointed Acting Secretary in his place at £50 a month, pending the return of Chapman from Odessa.

19 STC writes to WW to explain the loss of the important criticism of 'The Recluse', burnt among Major Adye's papers.

23 He visits some French and Spanish prisoners-of-war, working at repairing the roads. This rekindles his ardour for prison reform.

28 He visits his first government department, the local hospital, and is alienated by evidence of 'Catholic superstition'.

29   He issues his first document (*bando*) as Public Secretary.

February

3   (Sun) STC copies in his *Notebook* several of Shakespeare's sonnets about absence from the beloved. He also copies from the
Bible, 'O that thou wert as my Sister'.

5   John WW is drowned when his ship, the *Earl of Abergavenny*,
sinks off Portland Bill in a storm.

11 The WWs hear the news of John's death. WW trembles to
think of its effect on STC.

12 At 1.30 p.m. after a day of intense speculation and writing,
STC reaches an intellectual landmark: 'no Christ, no God, . . .
no Trinity, no God . . . Unitarianism in all its forms is idolatry.'
Thus he approaches the Trinitarianism which is to dominate
his last years.

13 STC accompanies Captain Pasley on a tour of the fortifications
on the far side of the harbour, which is new to him and which
impresses him deeply.

14 Mrs C at last hears from Malta that STC has become Ball's
'confidential secretary'. WW decides, since STC seems much
better, to write to him of John's death. 'I am sure he will return
the first minute he can after hearing the news.'

March

27 (Wed) The WWs receive a letter from STC saying he will
return in March. From now on, his friends await news of his
arrival in England.

28 STC visits another hospital near Floriana.

31 Lady Ball abruptly breaks the news to STC of John WW's
death. STC suffers deeply, but later over-dramatises his reaction in a letter to Mrs C in which he speaks of falling back in a
'convulsive hysteric fit'. Ball gives him two days off to recover
in the country.

April

4   (Thurs) STC writes adoringly again of Sara H and the 'grandeur of loving the Supreme in her'.

18 He meets Sarah Stoddart, who had received a letter from
Mary Lamb speaking of John WW's death and urging STC
to return to England. She also has heard from Mary of the
deaths of John Tobin the playwright, 'just after the success of

his Play!' and of STC's earliest schoolfellow at Christ's Hospital, Robert Allen.

23   He interviews the captain of a Turkish fleet which has entered Valletta.

*c.*26   He draws up a plan for a return journey overland (because of his terror of another sea voyage) via Messina, Rome, Venice and Vienna.

By the end of the month STC is drinking heavily to cope with the stress and is afraid of degenerating into 'a sot'.

May

1   (Wed) STC writes to Stuart of his financial affairs (he had written a briefer version on 30 April); he has saved £130 out of his salary. He is going to try to get a bill for £90 to Mrs C, but asks Stuart to lend her £50 if this bill should not arrive.

(mid)   STC draws up a project of a poem on Andalusia, his favourite romantic region.

June

(early)   STC seems to have helped quell a demonstration in Malta against the Jews.

July

10   (Wed) Tom Wedgwood dies. (In his will he has provided for half of STC's annuity to be paid annually to him for the rest of his life.) Mrs C withholds the news from STC, fearing an emotional reaction. Stuart sends her £50, as STC had requested him.

(end)   STC writes to Mrs C that Malta is 'dreary' and that he is determined to leave at the end of August. He is still awaiting the return of Chapman to take over his job. WW puts off a tour with Beaumont in expectation of STC's imminent arrival.

August

STC is taking opium and analysing the consequent visions in his *Notebooks*.

September

2   (Mon) STC issues his last '*bando*', against sheltering deserters on the island.

6   Chapman at long last returns to Malta and STC is free to go, once Chapman's fortnight of quarantine is over.
23   STC leaves Malta.
24   He reaches Syracuse.
26   He is again the guest of Mr and Mrs Leckie at their house on the site of Timoleon's Villa.
30   He travels to Catania with a servant and some mules to carry luggage.

October
3   (Thurs) He leaves Catania and travels, probably with Colin Mackenzie, the topographer, round the foot of Mount Etna.
4   The party reaches Messina.
21   STC's birthday. The Battle of Trafalgar and death of Nelson. STC still at Messina because of the worsening international situation. He seems to have decided to return to Syracuse with a British expedition, possibly to obtain passage for Naples via Augusta.
During this month Derwent stays with Sara H at Park House near Penrith – to his great improvement, says DW.

November
20   (Wed) STC arrives in Naples (probably with the British troops). He sees Vesuvius and is reminded of Skiddaw in the Lake District.

December
1   (Sun) STC travels to Salerno on an excursion down the Apennines.
14   Back to Naples, where the city is in mourning for the death of Nelson. At home Mrs C and the WWs are very anxious on hearing that STC intends to travel home overland, as Bonaparte is advancing through Europe.
18   News reaches Naples of Bonaparte's victory over the Austrians and Russians at Austerlitz: he can now turn his attention to avenging himself on Italy. Yet at this point STC accepts an invitation from a 'Mr B.' to go to Rome. At home, Sara H has hurried to Grasmere, believing that STC is about to return; WW is working at 'The Recluse', although DW observes: 'I do not think he will be able to do much till we have heard from Coleridge.'

25 STC sets off for Rome.
26 Reaches Gaeta.
31 Reaches Piazza di Spagna, near Rome.

1806

January

1 (Wed) STC has heard that the French army is expected in Rome on 5th. 'To stay or not to stay?' he asks himself. He decides to stay.
He sends his box of papers back to Naples to avoid interception by the French. He enjoys good company in Rome, which is full of artists under the patronage of Wilhelm von Humboldt, the Prussian minister. STC meets the German poet Ludwig Tieck and translates one of his love lyrics. He also meets the Scottish painter, George Wallis, and his young son, Trajan, whom STC thinks of as a prodigy.

February

15 (Sat) STC to Olevano with Washington Allston, a young American painter who is a close friend of Wallis.

March

2 (Sun) Bonaparte demands the expulsion of British subjects from papal territory. Meanwhile STC blithely enjoys the Apennines in spring.

April

3 (Thurs) STC to St Peter's in Rome to see the Maundy Thursday celebrations.
4 To the Sistine Chapel on Good Friday to see Michelangelo's *Last Judgement*.
STC is now short of money, but is helped out by a young Exeter artist, Thomas Russell.

May

(early) Wallis takes STC into his house, where he lapses into despondency over his opium dependency.
4 (Sun) To Rome for the beatification of a Jesuit. He still finds the Catholicism alien to him.

13 At home RS complains of STC's silence to his family and friends, although he has been heard about via several returned travellers.

18 STC leaves Rome for Florence. He later dramatises his journey by saying 'an order for my arrest was sent from Paris'. In fact, all British travellers were ordered to leave.

(end) Reaches Florence.

June

Travels to Pisa through Arno, 'a heavenly country'.

7 (Sat) Reaches Leghorn with Russell. They stay at the 'Arms of England' hotel. STC falls into despondency (perhaps at the prospect of another long sea-voyage?) and declares that it would have been better if he had died instead of John. At home, Sara H is still with the WWs and they have bound the copy of *The Prelude* she has made for STC. The WWs still plan to move to a bigger house, but don't want to make a decision until STC returns.

10 STC and Russell return to Florence, where they wait in vain for Wallis.

22 Back to Pisa.

23 STC reaches Leghorn, where he boards the *Gosport* and sets sail for home at last.

August

STC is very ill with opium symptoms during the journey and is cared for by Russell and Captain Derkheim. In a letter to Stuart he says that the ship was boarded by a Spanish privateer who forced Derkheim to throw overboard many papers, including some belonging to STC. Two *Notebooks* and *Observations on Egypt* survived. [STC had already left some papers in Malta and sent some back to his friend Noble in Naples. He thus reaches home without '9/10s', he says, of the manuscripts which he intended to use for his income.]

11 (Mon) STC is in quarantine off Plymouth.

17 He lands at Stangate Creek in Kent 'a little after ten' at night and offers up a prayer at a 'curious little chapel'.

18 He writes to Daniel Stuart, saying he will call on him soon. News that STC is in England reaches WW, who cancels a tour with Scott.

20 He writes to RS ('I write to you rather than to Mrs Coleridge because I can write more tranquilly'), ending: 'I will come as

soon as I can come.' STC goes on to the Bell Inn in London and calls on Lamb. He writes a note to WW, but with no indication of when he is to be expected in the north. Stuart offers him the use of his house in Brompton while he is away in Margate and lends him another £20.

September

8   (Mon) WW writes to Beaumont that STC does not wish to meet his wife again. STC is travelling between Parndon in Essex (home of MP William Smith), Margate and London. He sees the Clarksons, who are staying with Smith, and probably goes to Newmarket.

13 STC moves to the *Courier* offices in the Strand. His sonnet 'Farewell to Love' is published in the *Courier* this month.

16 STC's first letter to his wife since his return, written apparently at Mary Lamb's insistence. He pleads much business in London to excuse his delay. 'I feel with deep tho' sad affection toward you.'

18 WW writes to STC suggesting that they meet in London.

26 He writes again, having heard from Mrs C, saying he will have to stay on in London for a few days to meet Lord Howick.

28 WW has heard that STC will be in Keswick in a day or two. Sir George Beaumont has offered the WWs Hall Farmhouse at Coleorton in Leicestershire for six months; in the absence of any news from STC, WW has decided to accept the offer.

29 Another letter to Mrs C. STC says he is 'fretted out of all patience', but he still has not managed to see Lord Howick and will have to stay on longer to do so.

October

2   (Tues) STC writes again to Mrs C, bemoaning the delay in his return home. He has 'a doleful tale to relate': Captain Durkheim had promised to clear STC's possessions through Customs, but he has sailed again without doing so. STC has been in vain to Tower Hill in search of his belongings; he then sets George Fricker to the task. [The luggage is eventually retrieved by Russell and Clarkson in mid-October.]

3   Another letter to Mrs C: he is negotiating to give lectures at both the Royal and the London Institutes. [WW and RS are equally strongly against this idea.]

9   STC, still in London, is writing to Mrs C's brother George, who has visited him several times, about the nature of Christian faith.

*c.*10   STC is at the Clarksons in Bury St Edmunds. He is working on religious essays, pursuing his reconversion from Unitarianism to Trinitarianism.

23   (Thurs) STC leaves Bury St Edmunds hoping to meet Sara H at Penrith.

26   He misses her by half and hour; she travels on to join the WWs at Kendal and STC follows her there, arriving at the inn where they are staying at 7 in the evening. DW finds him very changed, fat and without 'the divine expression of his countenance'.

28   MW, DW and the children leave in the morning for Coleorton.

29   WW and Sara H leaves STC at 9 a.m. for Coleorton. They have discussed the possibility of staying at Grasmere or taking a house near Hawkshead, so as to remain near STC, but he won't hear of it. He explains his decision to separate from his wife and promises to join them at Coleorton in a month.

30   STC finally returns to Greta Hall after an absence of almost three years.

November

4   (Tues) STC presents Hartley with a Greek grammar book he has compiled from cuttings and from his own ideas.

7   WW writes to STC to urge him not to give lectures in London as he had planned, but to join them in Leicestershire.

*c.*19   STC writes to the WWs that he and his wife have determined to part 'absolutely and finally'. The boys will remain with STC but visit their mother in the holidays 'as they would do if at public school'.

December

21   STC and Hartley arrive at Coleorton, STC 'more like his old self', having, says DW, 'settled things at home to his satisfaction'. The old circle is complete for Christmas. STC is writing passionately in his *Notebooks* of Sara H – 'I know you love me' – and is beginning to feel jealousy of her admiration for WW. At the same time he writes to his wife of Hartley's good behaviour, saying that Sara H 'takes upon her all the duties of his mother & darling Friend, with all the Mother's love and fondness'.

1807

January

7 (Wed) WW reads *The Prelude* to STC. (Much of it was written during STC's time in Malta.) STC in response writes 'To William Wordsworth'.

During these weeks he walks often with the WWs and with Sara H, and his jealousy of WW's hold on the latter's affection grows. His manner changes enough for WW to write 'A Complaint'.

24 DW tells Lady Beaumont that STC does not take such strong stimulants as before.

February

(early) STC hopes that RS will move south with his family, taking Mrs C with him, and that the WWs may be able to take Greta Hall, since they are eager to return to the north. He himself would stay with the WWs. [When Mrs C hears of this idea she is 'almost frantic'.]

7 (Sat) He writes to Derwent with fatherly advice about loving his parents (especially his mother) and telling the truth.

March

3 (Tues) STC writes a poem to Derwent about poetic metre (later published).

Some time this month Mrs C and the children leave Greta Hall on a visit to Mrs Fricker in Bristol.

April

2 (Mon) STC writes to his brother George explaining his decision to separate from his wife, crediting her fairly with 'many excellent qualities, of strict modesty, attention to her children, and economy', but declaring that her 'temper and general tone of feeling . . . I have found wholly incompatible with even an endurable Life'.

3 He writes a letter for Hartley, advising him on his behaviour on a projected visit to his uncle George in Ottery: 'a grain of Honesty is better than a pound of Wit.'

STC, Hartley, Sara H and the WWs are in London for a month, staying first at the Montagus in Thornhaugh Street and later with Christopher W in Lambeth. STC is ill for much of the time. He does, however, meet Walter Scott at last. Scott and WW take Hartley to see the Tower of London.

18 (Sat) STC writes to Sotheby, saying he has read Sotheby's poem 'Saul' to 'a large company, where W. Wordsworth was present'. With a few alterations, he thinks, 'you will have established your Saul as the best epic poem in our language.'

30 He asks Godwin to rescue the only extant copy of *Osorio* from 'any chance rubbish-corner, in which it may have been preserved'. [This Godwin does, to STC's delight.] STC is still indignant at Sheridan's rejection of his play.

May

4 (Mon) STC sees Sara H off on the coach to the Clarksons at Bury St Edmunds.

5 He asks Sotheby for an advance of £50 for two months. [Sotheby obliges at once.]

STC and Hartley set off later in the month for Bristol, where Mrs C has been awaiting him for two months at her sister Martha's.

June

6 (Sat) STC and family to Poole's at Nether Stowey, on their way, as they think, to Ottery. This is an important visit for STC: he is taking Mrs C to see his family 'as a debt of respect to her for her many praiseworthy qualities' – in other words, as a public declaration that their separation is not to be seen as a slur upon her. However, having been ill, he has not opened his brother George's letter of 6 April. When he does, he discovers that George cannot receive him at Ottery because of family illness. STC feels this as a betrayal: he had gone to the expense of the visit to the West Country expressly to take the children to see his family.

25 STC writes at last to Josiah Wedgwood (his first letter to him since his return from Malta), expressing his sorrow at Tom Wedgwood's death and excusing himself for not having written earlier. He speaks of having finished a Greek/English grammar and of working on a Greek/English lexicon.

July

STC enjoys his stay with Poole, despite suffering symptoms of gout and spraining his leg while climbing over a high hedge; he visits Lord Egremont at Enmore, the Brices at Ainsholt and the Chubbs at Bridgwater. Thomas De Quincey, who wants to make his acquaintance, visits Poole for two days, then goes on to Bridgwater where he

finally catches up with STC. STC probably writes 'Recollections of
Love' during this stay in Stowey.
30   (Thurs) Mrs C and the children leave for Bristol, escorted by
     De Quincey.

September
STC writes to Mary Cruikshank, defending his political views: even
in his youth, he asserts, they were 'decidedly anti-jacobin, and anti-
revolutionary'. For the last ten years he has been 'fighting inces-
santly' against French expansionism.
(early)   After receiving an invitation from Humphrey Davy, STC
begins to plan a winter lecture course for the Royal Institution on
'Poetry and the Principle of Taste', illustrated by Shakespeare,
Spenser, Milton, Dryden, Pope and modern poets.
Later in the month he rejoins Mrs C and the family in Bristol, much
better in health after the stay with Poole.

October
(end)   Mrs C and the children return to Keswick, again escorted by
De Quincey, while STC prepares to set off for London to arrange his
lectures. However, he falls ill and has to stay in Bristol, where he is
looked after by John Morgan, his wife and sister Charlotte. [He has
been acquainted with the family since his early days in Bristol, and
there is the suspicion of an attachment to Charlotte.] De Quincey,
through Cottle, arranges an anonymous gift of £300 to STC, which
STC agrees to accept as a loan.

November
23   (Mon) STC finally arrives in London, but Davy's serious ill-
     ness delays the lectures.

December
14   (Mon) STC writes to RS, horror-struck at Davy's illness –
     'after discoveries more intellectual . . . than Newton's! But he
     must not die!' He also mentions having read Scott's 'The Lay
     of the Last Minstrel', which others had felt to have been based
     on 'Christabel'; however, he sees no likeness at all.
18   He writes to Richard Sharp MP asking if he can find a place in
     an almshouse for the worthy widow of D. Brewman, a printer.
     She had been nurse at Christ's Hospital when he was an upper
     boy there: 'from her I received the greatest tenderness, a ten-

derness which, God knows! I had never received before, even
from my own family' [see September 1789].
STC returns twice to Bristol during this month while waiting for the
lectures to be arranged.

28　DW explains in a letter to Mrs Clarkson that they had rented
Allan Bank on the assumption that STC would join them and
live there with Hartley and Derwent; they would not like him
now, except as an occasional visitor.

1808

January

12　(Tues) STC spends the evening at a glee club, where he much
enjoys the music.

13　He takes a six-month lease on rooms lent him by Stuart at the
Courier office.

15　Disastrous beginning to the lectures at the Royal Institution on
'Poetry and the Principles of Taste': STC is ill and can scarcely
leave his bed.

22　He has to put off the next lecture because of continuing illness;
'I disappoint some hundreds!'

February

During this month STC's letters, especially to the Morgans, are full
of misery and details of his physical ailments.

2　(Tues) STC writes to De Quincey in great detail about his own
poor health.

5　DW records that the only good news of STC is that he has
begun the lectures. She is sure he still takes opiates.

9　STC writes miserably to RS, 'I know, that I have not many
months to live.'

10　He is moved by a visit from his old school-friend, Thomas
Middleton, now a Greek scholar.

By the end of this month STC has given only two lectures. De
Quincey, who has come to London to take notes of the lectures,
records that on two occasions STC simply did not turn up, to the
annoyance of his audience.

18　STC writes to Daniel Stuart and to Sir George Beaumont asking for their help in releasing Sara H's brother Henry, taken up
by a pressgang.

23 WW leaves for London, hoping to return with STC, whose physical condition, he is convinced, is the result of opium.

March

29 (Tues) STC reveals in letters to the Morgans and to RS his great anxiety about Sara H who is ill at Dove Cottage with inflammation of the lungs.

April

The lectures are now continuing regularly. WW has attended twice.

3 (Sun) WW leaves London, seen off by STC at 7 a.m. when the city is covered in snow [see 'On Westminster Bridge']. He has left the manuscript of 'The White Doe of Rylstone' with STC for him to negotiate publication with Longman.

4 STC regrets not being able to see Mathilda Betham, the miniature painter, who wishes to paint his portrait. [She eventually paints him in 1811.]

5? He meets Mary Evans (now Mrs Todd) at the Royal Institution and later calls upon her and her husband. She too is unhappily married, and he sees in her fate 'a counterpart of the very worst parts of my own Fate, in an exaggerated Form'.

*c.*18 He asks Daniel Stuart for a loan of £100. [He is anxious to pay his insurance policy, due on 7 April.] He also writes to Stuart with detailed advice about choosing a wife – 'the most important step of human Life'.

May

STC is preparing WW's poem 'The White Doe of Rylstone' for the press. WWs move this month to Allan Bank.

1 (Sun) STC writes a long answer to the Duke of Sussex about Johann P. Palm's pamphlet, *The Spirit of the Times* (for which Bonaparte has had Palm executed); is interrupted by seven people calling on him in succession. Dines at 5 p.m. with a Mr Barnard and a group of people gathered especially to meet him.

2 After a similar day, dines at 6 p.m. with the Bishop of Durham.

3 Gives an extra double lecture (that is, over two hours) on education, adding a defence of his friend Andrew Bell and an attack on the Quaker Joseph Lancaster. [This is very controversial and the proprietors of the Institution take offence.] Dines with the Literary Fund (though he goes at first by mistake to the Whig Club, to everyone's embarrassment).

4   Gives another lecture of over an hour. Dines with the 'famous Rout-giving, over-rich Mr and Mrs Thompson in Portman Square'.

5   Prepares lecture for tomorrow. Writes to Mrs C, apologising for delay in writing and giving the account of the week's activities (as above) to explain how busy he is.

7   STC tries to meet Mathilda Betham, but leaves behind her address and cannot find her.

10 STC sends an apology to the organisers of the lectures: he has fallen while getting out of a boat, after crossing the Thames from Vauxhall to Somerset House, and hurt his head.
He has negotiated terms with Longman for the publication of WW's 'White Doe'. WW, however, eventually decides not to publish the poem, which elicits a long protesting letter from STC. Another letter follows (of which only WW's reply survives), accusing WW of too close a friendship with Charles Lloyd, of taking sides with Stoddart (with whom STC has quarrelled), and most of all, of attempting to discourage Sara H's feelings for him.

11 STC writes to brother George for a copy of his birth certificate (presumably in connection with increasing his insurance), and pours out his bitterness at George's refusal to see him and the family on the trip to Devon. [George's reply shows that his motive was that he considered STC's separating from Mrs C 'an irreligious act'.]

21 In a letter to WW, STC mentions for the first time the idea of producing a new periodical [later called the *Friend*]. He has sent a prospectus to Sotheby and Sir George Beaumont.

June

13 (Mon) STC writes to the Secretary of the Royal Institution explaining that illness forces him to abandon the lectures. [He has given eighteen lectures and earned £100. Subsequent letters indicate that the members of the Royal Institution continued to admire and respect him.] He then leaves London for the Clarksons at Bury St Edmunds.

July

STC writes of Sara H to Daniel Stuart, praising her 'Sense, Sensibility, Sweetness of Temper, perfect Simplicity and . . . unpretending Nature'. STC's review of Thomas Clarkson's *History of the Abolition of the Slave Trade* appears in the *Edinburgh Review*.

September

1   (Thurs) STC visits the WWs at Allan Bank for the first time.
5   STC to Keswick with WW who has to be out of the house while MW is confined.
6   Catharine W born.
7   STC and WW return to Allan Bank with little Sara, who is a great favourite, particularly beloved by John W.

Hartley and Derwent are this month placed in the Reverend John Dawes's school at Ambleside, but spend Saturdays and Sundays at Allan Bank.

19 In a letter to T. G. Street, co-proprietor of the *Courier*, STC discusses his attempts to break free from opium. He comments on its widespread use: 'Throughout Lancashire and Yorkshire it is the common Dram of the lower orders of People.' STC, WW and Sara H travel in the Duddon Valley. STC meets John Wilson ('Christopher North' of *Blackwood's Magazine*) who has a house at Elleray.

December

STC at Allan Bank working at the *Friend*. William Savage, of the Royal Institution, is to be publisher. STC and the WWs send out prospectuses, including batches to RS and Poole to distribute, and one to brother George.

4   (Sun) STC writes to Poole asking him to begin 'to count my Life, as a Friend of your's [*sic*], from 1 January, 1809'.
c.4 He writes to Daniel Stuart that the *Friend* is written, not for the multitude, but for the men who will influence the multitude.

1809

January

STC, full of good resolutions, works with Daniel Stuart at launching the *Friend*. Sara H is his amanuensis and when she is ill during this month he cannot work. He mourns the death of Dr Thomas Beddoes, which moved him, he says, even more than the death of Tom Wedgwood.

February

5   (Sun) STC to Kendal, where he learns that 'Old Mr Pennington', whom he relied upon to print the *Friend*, is about to go into

retirement.
8 He writes to John Monkhouse in Penrith to ask John Brown, the printer there, if he will take over the printing of the *Friend*.
10 Tom Hutchinson and John Monkhouse buy a farm in Radnorshire.
12 STC leaves Allan Bank for Penrith, via Grisdale where he sprains his knee while jumping a brook. He visits John Brown the publisher and arranges 1 April for the first issue of the *Friend*.

March
STC is at home in Keswick with mumps for part of this month, but is otherwise active in preparing the *Friend* for publication. He travels between Keswick, Penrith and Appleby, where he stays with J. C. Curwen of Workington Hall; he persuades him to use his powers as an MP to frank the whole postage of the first issue of the *Friend*.

April
1 (Sat) At Appleby papers are signed with Mr Wilkin, Distributor of Stamps, for the publication of the *Friend*. Present are STC, John Brown the printer, and WW and RS, who have agreed to stand as first and second securities.

May
1 (Mon) STC intends another visit to Penrith but is ill in Keswick for several days.
5 He reports the arrival of '1250 of Stamped Paper' from Stuart in London for the first edition of the *Friend*. WW writes to encourage him always to be beforehand with his work on the *Friend*.
Some time this month STC stays for a week with Thomas Wilkinson of Yanwath, WW's Quaker friend. Here he is kept without stimulants and he returns restored. (DW later says that TW was 'the Father of *The Friend*'.)
25 WW is in correspondence with Daniel Stuart and writes dismissively of STC's efforts over the *Friend*: he 'is not sufficiently master of his own efforts to execute anything which requires a regular course of application to one object'.
*c.*30 WW writes to Poole that he has no confidence in STC's 'moral constitution'. He has been three weeks at Penrith without writing. WW hopes the *Friend* will not appear.

June

1 (Thurs) First number of the *Friend* appears.
4 WW writes to Stuart, '*The Friend* has at last appeared. I am sorry for it as I have not the least hope that it can proceed.'
8 Second number of the *Friend*.
13 STC returns to Allan Bank after nearly four months away.
15 WW now writes to Stuart much more hopefully of STC's resolution, encouraging Stuart to help with paper.

July

STC says he is getting up at 5 a.m. and working for three hours before breakfast.
7 (Fri) Stuart writes that another 2500 stamped sheets of paper are on their way. This, he estimates, should cover the first eight numbers.
(late) STC sends off material for the third and fourth numbers of the *Friend*.

August

10 (Thurs) Third number of the *Friend*. There are still problems with supplies of paper. STC has misunderstood Stuart and thinks, wrongly, that he promised to pay for paper for the first ten numbers.

September

7 (Thurs) Fourth number of the *Friend*.
14 Fifth number.
(mid) William Jackson, STC's 'Friend & Landlord', of Greta Hall, dies. He leaves his favourite, Hartley, £50 when he comes of age.
18 Sara H, though still in poor health, is busy transcribing both for the *Friend* and for WW.
21 Sixth number.
28 Seventh number.

October

5 (Thurs) STC sends off as many copies of the eighth number of the *Friend* as he has paper for.
9 STC writes angrily to Stuart about the situation over the paper. [Although in fact Stuart has spent £104 on paper for the *Friend*, STC thinks he has cancelled out this debt by contributing eight 'Letters on the Spaniards' to the *Courier* for him.]

12   Ninth number of the *Friend* due to appear, but delayed be-
     cause (says RS), 'The rats eat [*sic*] up the motto at the printer's.'
     It appears a few days later.
20   STC writes despondently to RS of his fears that 'the plan and
     execution of the *Friend* is so utterly unsuitable to the public
     taste as to preclude all rational hopes of its success'.
STC writes to Tom Hutchinson, Richard Sharp, Poole, and his brother
George, asking them to share the cost of the *Friend* up to the twentieth number. All agree, except George Coleridge, which leads to
further estrangement between STC and his family.
*c.*19 Tenth number.
26   Eleventh number.

November
2   (Thurs) The *Friend* fails to appear – but otherwise it runs
     regularly until the end of the year.
4   Death of STC's mother. George C writes to STC before and
     after the event but receives no reply. [STC writes to RS before
     the death, bemoaning the fact that George, though he 'knows
     I am penniless', has offered him no money to go to Ottery.]
9   Twelfth number of the *Friend* – 'a most brilliant one', writes
     Stuart, though it is a week late.
10   Stuart sends paper, unsolicited, but this is his final contribu-
     tion to the *Friend*.
16, 23, 30   Thirteenth, fourteenth and fifteenth numbers of the *Friend*.

December
STC's articles on Spanish politics begin to appear in the *Courier*.
7   (Thurs) Sixteenth number of the *Friend*.
14   Seventeenth number.
21   (Thurs) Eighteenth number.
25   STC, the WWs and De Quincey spend Christmas Day with
     John Wilson in his cottage at Elleray.

1810

January
4   (Thurs) Twentieth number of the *Friend*. After this, sub-
     scribers will have to pay. Subscriptions arrive slowly and
     are inadequate.

11   Supernumerary number of the *Friend*, asking subscribers to pay at their local post offices. STC declares his aim to achieve a more light-hearted tone, in response to the complaints of friends and correspondents.

31   Twenty-second number.

February

8   (Thurs) Twenty-third number.

15   Twenty-fourth number.

19?   (Mon) STC writes proudly to his wife about their sons. Derwent (because of his yellow smock and small size) was called Stumpy Canary ('li'l Darren' to the country people), but both are now schoolboys and quite grown-up, discussing 'the present state of Agriculture in France' during their weekend at Allen Bank.

22   Twenty-fifth number of the *Friend*. DW writes that STC, who 'either does a great deal or nothing at all', has been writing with a speed which is 'truly astonishing'. He dictates to Sara H, often completing a number of the *Friend* in two days. John Monkhouse, Tom Hutchinson's partner in the Welsh farm, is staying at Grasmere, recovering from an injury caused when his horse kicked him.

March

1   (Thurs) Twenty-sixth number of the *Friend*.

15   The last issue of the *Friend* (the twenty-eighth but called 27). Some time this month, or perhaps earlier, Sara H leaves for her brother's new farm at Hindwell, Radnorshire in Wales. She takes the opportunity of John Monkhouse's departure to travel with him. DW writes that STC especially 'will miss her, for she has transcribed almost every paper of *The Friend* for the press. She was the cause of the continuance of *The Friend* so long . . . (but) he was tired, and she had at last no power to drive him on.'

April

12   (Thurs) STC continues to talk as if the *Friend* were being published still.

May

2?   (Wed) STC leaves Allan Bank for Greta Hall, among other things to talk to his wife about Hartley's future. [He intends to stay ten days but in fact is at home for six months and never lives with the WWs again.]

June–August
STC is at home in Keswick. Mrs C writes to Poole that 'in all that time he has not appeared to be employed in composition': 'Poor Man! I have not the least doubt but he is the most unhappy of the two!' During this time he teaches his wife and daughter Italian.

September
23   (Sun) Basil Montagu arrives at Allan Bank with his third wife, whom WW dislikes. They visit Greta Hall and Montagu persuades STC to stay with them in London (55 Frith Street, Soho) and consult their physician, Anthony Carlisle, in an attempt to conquer opium addiction. WW feels that he must tell Montagu of STC's habits, to dissuade him from the arrangement; Montagu thereupon decides (according to DW) that STC should live in lodgings near him, rather than in his house, but nothing is said directly to STC.

October
(early) STC writes to WW pouring scorn on Scott's 'The Lady of The Lake' which he has at last read. (It came out in May.)
18   (Thurs) STC sets off for London with the Montagus.
26   They arrive in London.
28   During this Sunday evening, Montagu and STC quarrel (about wine, says De Quincey later) and Montagu tells STC about WW's warning. Crabb Robinson in his later account suggests that Montagu (falsely) says: 'WW has commissioned me to tell you – for years past you have been an Absolute Nuisance to the family.' STC moves out to Hudson's Hotel, Covent Garden, where he writes at length in his *Notebook* of his disillusionment with WW.
Montagu writes to tell WW of the quarrel; WW replies that he thinks Montagu has acted unwisely – but he writes nothing to STC.

November
Anthony Carlisle proves unprofessional and indiscreet and talks of STC's case to others. He even writes about him to RS, who says 'the case is utterly hopeless'.
1   (Thurs) STC writes to John Monkhouse praising Monkhouse's

sister, 'the only woman, of whom I ever heard WW deliver entire praise, & without any drawback, his own wife excepted'.

3 STC leaves Hudson's Hotel to live with the Morgans (7 Portland Place, Hammersmith). John Morgan has been told rumours of STC and realises that there are enemies at work against his character. [STC is based at the Morgans for more than a year.] On this day, STC writes on the manuscript of 'Kubla Khan' a note linking its composition with recourse to opium at the time of his quarrel with Charles Lloyd. [This leads E. H. Coleridge to date the poem May 1798.]

14 STC writes to John Rickman asking for the loan of Cobbett's latest numbers. He is apparently writing for the *Courier*.

15? STC writes to Godwin: 'I have been of late in a very low way.'

18 Supper at Godwin's.

During this month STC meets Henry Crabb Robinson for the first time; HCR records his conversation.

December

21 (Fri) STC writes to the Morgans from Brown's Coffee House, Mitre Court, Fleet Street: he is looking for lodgings near Gray's Inn and for a doctor to treat him. He has decided to write directly to Dr John Abernethy.

References to WW in STC's letters at this time could support the view that STC only gradually realises the extent of his hurt (see letter to Stuart, 28 April 1811). DW believes that the break is the result of STC's fancies and she hopes that 'they will die away of themselves'.

1811

January

29 (Tues) STC has dinner at John Rickman's with HCR and others. He talks (as HCR records) of Shakespeare's fools as supplying the place of the Greek chorus.

February

STC temporarily leaves the Morgans for 32/34 Southampton Buildings in the Strand. During this month George Burnett dies wretchedly in the Marylebone Infirmary.

March

(early) STC is shocked at Burnett's death.

8 (Fri) Mary Lamb, on the verge of a relapse herself, writes to WW begging him to come to Town immediately, as STC's mind is 'seriously unhinged' by news of Burnett's death. [WW does not take this news seriously: he has heard from the Montagus that STC is cheerful and 'has his hair dressed and powdered every day'.]

9 Mary Lamb is placed under confinement again.

10 STC to supper at Lady Jerningham's.

12 Writes to HCR about the state of being in Love. 'WW is by nature incapable of being in Love, though no man more tenderly attached.' Writes of Catherine Clarkson in warmest terms: 'She has all that is good in me, and of all that is innocent'; if he had had her as a sister, 'I should have been a great man'. He mourns that 'All my dearest Friends I have of late either suffered from or suffered for.'

29 STC at Hazlitt's with CL, HCR and others. He 'philosophised as usual', says HCR.

30 STC at CL's with HCR and Hazlitt. He speaks in defence of Godwin. They talk of national characteristics. STC has an antipathy to the Irish, but no aversion to Turks or Jews, says HCR.

During this month and the next, STC meets Henry Grattan, the Irish statesman, and Signora Catalina, the singer; he also at last meets Mathilda Betham, who paints a miniature of him (see 7 May 1808).

April

19 (Fri) STC's first contribution in a series of articles for the *Courier*. [This goes on from 7 May to 27 September with a big gap in June.]

20–21 STC is at Richmond at the home of John May, a friend of RS and of STC's brother, James; here he meets his own nephews, John Taylor Coleridge and Henry Nelson Coleridge, sons of James. John records the first of STC's conversations, and later publishes it in *Table Talk*. They go to the Royal Observatory where they meet Stephen Peter Rigaud, mathematical historian and astronomer.

28 STC writes to Stuart: 'so deep and rankling is the wound, which WW has wantonly and without the slightest provoca-

tion inflicted in return for fifteen years' most enthusiastic, self-despising and alas! self-injuring Friendship . . . that I cannot return to Grasmere.'

30 He sends three songs he has composed to John Whitaker, composer and music publisher, hoping they can be published.

May

2 (Thurs) STC writes to Thomas N. Longman, the publisher, with a proposal for a 'Volume of 360 pages'. [This comes to nothing.]

3 Arrangements have been made for STC to work regularly for the *Courier*. [He produces 45 prose contributions before 27 September.]

12 DW writes to Mrs Clarkson that the family now regularly go to church for the sake of the children, including Hartley and Derwent. WW has learnt from Mrs C how 'cruelly injured' STC feels at WW's betrayal in warning Montagu against him, but he will not write directly to STC until he hears from him personally.

28 HCR calls on STC, who talks of his own liberal opinions in politics.

Some time this summer, John Payne Collier meets STC.

June

6 (Thurs) At an art exhibition, STC meets HCR and criticises the 'vigorous impotence' of Fuseli's Macbeth.

11 STC reads HCR 'a very beautiful essay' criticising the reappointment of the Duke of York as commander-in-chief of the army, which the *Courier* has not printed – to STC's annoyance.

July

HCR approaches the proprietor of *The Times* on STC's behalf, but with no success. [STC had proposed that he should supply two essays a week and attend the office six hours a day.]

21 (Fri) HCR visits Charles Lamb; CL tells him that WW has treated STC with great unkindness.

24 HCR meets Southey at Lamb's; RS says of STC that, 'with a strong sense of duty, he has neglected it in every relation of life'.

August

3 (Sat) HCR 'chatted till 11' with Lamb, who angrily attacks his expression 'poor Coleridge': STC, he says, is a 'fine fellow'.

September

27 (Fri) STC's last *Courier* article.

October

5 (Sat) STC writes to T. G. Street saying that he has completed character studies of Pitt, Buonaparte, Fox and Sir A. Ball. [There is no evidence that he has.]

At the beginning of the month STC leaves the Morgans, hurt by their 'contempt' for his drinking and opium addiction. He lodges at 6 Southampton Buildings in the Strand.

12 STC writes to John Morgan explaining that he could not have told the Morgans the truth if he had stayed with them, because of the demands of the addiction. He speaks of his current difficulties, including 'clamorous letters' from Mrs C and 'the never-closing, festering Wound of Wordsworth & his Family'.

15 He writes again, apologising to the Morgans about his departure: 'It was intolerable to me to bring back to your Home of Peace and Love a spirit so disquieted.'

26 STC mentions to John Rickman his solicitude for CL, who is plagued with visits from Hazlitt. He worries that even his own company once a week may be injurious to CL's health. [CL himself never complains of STC however.]

30 HCR notes STC's plans for a course of fifteen lectures to be given in the Coachmakers' Hall during the winter.

November

18 (Mon) STC begins his lecture series, having moved the venue to Scot's Corporation Hall, Crane Court, Fleet Street. The subject is to be the English poets from Shakespeare and Milton to the present day. Byron and Samuel Rogers are among those who attend during the winter.

During this month STC suffers from severe bowel pains, but recovers in time to begin the lectures, which continue through November, December and January. In all STC gives seventeen rather than fifteen lectures. Dates in November: 18, 21, 25, 28.

December

STC's lectures are on 2, 5, 9, 12, 16, 19 and 30 of this month.

5 (Thurs) George Dawe the sculptor takes a mask of STC's features. [He exhibits the completed bust at the Royal Academy in 1812.] HCR thinks STC surpasses himself in his lecture: it is supposed to be on *Romeo and Juliet*, but instead STC talks of flogging in school and of the character of the age of Elizabeth and of James I. 'Incorrigible', says HCR.

9 STC's 'incomparably best' lecture, says HCR, on love in *Romeo and Juliet*.

30 HCR leaves STC's lecture early (he's drunk too much to listen properly), but says that STC was good, 'methodical and kept to his subject'.

During this month STC dines with John Rickman and spends an evening or two every week with Lamb.

1812

January

17 (Fri) STC at dinner at J. Buck's with HCR and others. He relates anecdotes against himself.

20 STC's lecture, continuing his discussion of Milton. HCR, Byron and Samuel Rogers in the audience. 'Not one of his happiest lectures', says HCR.

27 Last of STC's lecture series. Very well-attended. He develops the character of Milton's Satan, and attacks Mrs Barbauld's poetry, which shocks HCR in the audience as being 'unmanly'; he also analyses a description of moonlight in Pope's Homer.

Revival of public interest in the *Friend*: STC finds new publishers, John Gale and Thomas Curtis, and plans to reissue the old numbers.

February

10 (Mon) STC to Liverpool by coach: tries in vain to arrange a series of lectures there. Visits the Crompton family.

17 Spends a day in Kendal collecting the reprinted issues of the *Friend*.

18 Collects Hartley and Derwent from school but passes through Grasmere on the way home to Keswick without stopping at the WWs.

March

STC with his family in Keswick. Mrs C tells him that WW regards the quarrel as a trifle (though DW had hoped he would visit them at once on his arrival). He is delayed in Keswick by RS's reluctant departure to see the sick Charles Lloyd. STC needs to discuss things with RS before he leaves.

26 (Thurs) STC leaves for London via Penrith. He has made no effort to call on the WWs despite having received three letters in four days: 'I have been in such a state of fever and irritation about the Wordsworths, my reason deciding one way and my heart pulling me the contrary – scarcely daring to set off without seeing them, especially Miss Hutchinson who has done nothing to offend me.' [He never sees Grasmere or Keswick again.]

April

c.12 (Sun) WW sets off for London, hoping for a reconciliation with STC. STC, after being held up by snow for a week in Penrith, is now back with the Morgans at 71 Berners Street, Soho.

21 Writes to Mrs C about George Dawe (artist) who is visiting the Lake District: she is to 'receive him as a friend'. Asks if RS has read 'Childe Harold': 'all the world is talking of it'. STC has not read it, but says it sounds exactly like a plan he himself conceived six years ago.

24 Writes to Richard Sharp MP, describing WW as 'my bitterest Calumniator'. STC is planning to issue supplementary copies of the *Friend*, but needs WW's two last *Essays on Epitaphs*. He writes for them via Mrs C, but WW has already left for London. DW writes briefly to STC to tell him this. STC is planning another series of lectures on European Drama.

May

2 (Sat) Sharp gives STC's letter to WW on his arrival in London. [DW is later to quote from it bitterly.] WW tries to arrange a meeting through Charles Lamb, with Montagu present and with Josiah Wedgwood as arbitrator.

3 STC tells HCR that he will see WW, but not in the presence of Montagu. He is very emotional at losing such a friend as WW, says HCR.

4 STC writes to WW with a long account of his feelings (includ-

ing a defence of his wearing powder and being in high spirits!) and concluding that he still loves WW. WW does not open the letter. Lamb, despairing at the coldness between them, takes no further part in the affair.

8   WW calls on Henry Crabb Robinson and asks him to visit STC, which he does without delay. He notes that STC shows much more feeling than WW. STC repeats that he is willing to see WW, but not in the presence of Montagu. WW returns a message, clarifying what he said to Montagu in September 1810. According to HCR, WW (a) denies having given Montagu any message for STC: what he said to Montagu was for 'friendly purpose only'; (b) denies ever having used the phrase 'rotten drunkard'; (c) denies having called STC a 'Nuisance to the family'; (d) says he does not want to confront him and Montagu, but hopes STC will simply take him at his word. He also tells HCR that STC's mental powers are 'greater than those of any man he ever knew'. He says he is willing to see STC, but not alone. [He fears STC's emotionalism.]

10 Josiah Wedgwood offers to act as mediator (though he has not seen STC for seven years). HCR visits STC and collects a statement of facts from him for WW.

11 Assassination of Prime Minister Spencer Perceval in the House of Commons. HCR visits WW, who prepares a reply to STC's statement, trying not to hurt STC's feelings. HCR comments in his diary that he prefers 'the coolness of such a man to the heat of C.'. HCR visits STC but he is out. He revisits him in the evening. STC is shocked at the assassination and speaks favourably and emotionally of Perceval. He whispers to HCR that WW's reply is quite satisfactory and that he has answered it immediately.

13 WW breakfasts with William Lisle Bowles. He considers that a reconciliation has been achieved between himself and STC.

17 STC dines at the Beaumonts' with WW, Washington Allston and David Wilkie, the artist (who painted Hartley's portrait in 1807).

19 STC's first lecture at Willis' Rooms (aimed at an aristocratic audience). He compares classic and romantic drama. [The lectures last till 5 June.] HCR reports that WW and STC have now met several times but that neither has mentioned the quarrel.

22 WW dines with STC and the Morgans.

23 Lady Beaumont arranges for a large group of friends, including WW, to attend STC's lecture.

29 WW again attends STC's lecture, as does HCR, who feels STC confuses mythology, metaphysics and so on. WW, STC and HCR talk together afterwards at Morgan's. STC talks of the impossibility of being a good poet without being a good man. He agrees with Kant, but says he has gained no new ideas from Schelling.

30 WW calls on STC and they have a pleasant walk to Hampstead together. [This is possibly their only time alone.]

During this month George Dawe paints STC's portrait.

June
During this month the *Friend* is reissued by Gale and Curtis.

4 (Thurs) Catharine W dies of convulsions at the age of three.

5 STC's last lecture of his course. HCR reports that he 'promised to speak of *Othello*, but wasted time instead on *The Winter's Tale*'. The lectures have not been a financial success, attracting only 50 subscribers.

10 News of the child's death reaches WW, who walks to tell HCR. They go together to STC, stopping at De Quincey's on the way. (De Q bursts into tears at the news.) WW leaves for Wales to break the news to his wife. The reconciliation with STC has been achieved, but it seems that STC's feeling for WW (and for DW and Sara H?) has gone.

August
7 (Fri) After a long gap in which STC seems to have written few letters, he writes to Stuart: he has been ill with suspected dropsy; a new doctor, Robert Gooch, is attending him. He recommends a reduction in opiates. STC offers Stuart some articles and asks for a loan. Stuart sends him £20.

13 STC has several hours' talk with HCR. STC admits Goethe's genius but bemoans his lack of 'religion and enthusiasm'. He praises *Wallenstein*, but criticises Schiller for 'ventriloquism in poetry'.

October
Osorio rechristened *Remorse*, is accepted for early production at Drury Lane.

November
This month STC and RS jointly publish *Omniana*, a two-volume scrapbook of miscellaneous pieces.
3 (Tues) STC begins a series of twelve lectures at the Surrey Institute. HCR attends, but finds the material familiar – Shakespeare, Milton – and the lecture dull. Afterwards STC walks back to HCR's rooms. Borrows and kisses a copy of Spinoza: the book is his gospel (despite S's false philosophy).
9 Josiah Wedgwood writes to STC that because of wartime financial losses he now has to pay STC's annuity out of capital rather than income and does not feel able to continue unless STC feels him 'bound in honour to do so'.
17 HCR again at STC's lecture, but falls asleep.
STC's lectures continue on 10, 17 and 24 at the Surrey Institute.

December
1 (Tues) Death of Thomas Wordsworth, STC's favourite of the WW children. STC writes to Josiah Wedgwood, releasing him from his bond with dignity and gratitude. [Thomas Wedgwood's half of the annuity was left in his will for STC for life but, after tax, is under £75.]
7 STC, having heard of Thomas's death from WW, writes back emotionally, but still will not visit him, although DW has also written to beg him to come.
Lectures continue at the Surrey Institute on 1 and 8.

1813

January
On 5, 12, 19 and 26 STC's lectures continue at the Surrey Institute.
23 (Sat) *Remorse* is produced at Drury Lane and is well-received. [It runs for twenty performances, which is a good run by the standards of the time.] STC is able to send his wife £100 and the promise of another £100. (In all, says HCR, he makes £400 from the play.) [W. Pople, the printer, issues three editions of *Remorse* during this year.]
26 STC is loudly applauded at the beginning and end of his last lecture.

February

13 (Sat) STC writes affectionately to Poole (from whom he seems to have had a temporary estrangement). He speaks of his gladness at not having the Wedgwood annuity: now he knows that his love for Josiah is genuine, and not merely based on gratitude: 'To Mr Thomas Wedgwood I felt, doubtless, Love; but it was mingled with Fear . . . But Josiah – O I ever did, & ever shall, love him, as a Being so beautifully balanced in mind & heart deserves to be.'

20 He dines with George Caldwell ('my earliest College Friend').

March

2 (Tues) HCR and Charles Aders visit STC, who talks of music and of his hero, Purcell. He says he prefers Goethe's earlier works, especially *Werther*, to the later ones; he criticises Schiller for narrowness in his exclusive admiration of Shakespeare.

11 Catherine Clarkson tracks STC down in London, with the help of HCR, but cannot persuade him to come north. [From this point she becomes disillusioned with him and fades out of his life.]

13 STC and John Morgan, who is ill, go to the seaside (Bexhill, Sussex) for a few days for Morgan's health. The WWs are disappointed that STC has not visited them, despite his repeated promises after the death of Thomas. He has ignored their letters.

April

8 (Thurs) DW writes to Catherine Clarkson that STC 'will not let himself be served by others' and will not let himself see 'that we have always loved him, do still love him'. She no longer wishes him to come north if it is only to gratify them, but hopes that he may come of his own free will. [He never does.]

August

The Morgan family are bankrupt. John Morgan has lost the large inheritance left him by his father and invested in a cheesemongery business and in Brent & Co., tobacconists. The Morgans move to 19 London Street, Fitzroy Square. STC exerts himself to help them.

September
John Morgan flees to Ireland while his affairs are sorted out. STC pawns his books [presumably to help the Morgans].
 2   (Thurs) STC meets Madame de Stael.

October
 4   (Mon) DW writes of Hartley's increasing eccentricity and need for a new school; she does not expect help from STC.
 21   STC at Bristol, staying at the home of his old friend Josiah Wade, the linen-draper (2 Queen's Square). He is working hard to sort out the affairs of John Morgan, and arranges for a cheque for £100 to be sent to Morgan's creditors.
 28   STC gives the first of a series of lectures, six on Shakespeare and two on education.

November
STC's lectures continue on Tuesdays and Thursdays, 2, 4, 9, 11, 16, 18 and 23 of this month.
 2   (Tues) Robert Southey takes the oath as Poet Laureate. STC writes querulously to Mrs Morgan and Charlotte that they should write to him every other day. He is especially worried about Mrs Morgan's health.
 14   He writes to the Morgans that he would like to find lodgings for himself and them somewhere in Bristol.
 24   STC returns to London at the end of his lecture series.
 29   He sets off for Bath, taking Mrs Morgan and Charlotte into the country for the sake of the former's health.

December
 5   (Sun) STC lodges the sisters at Ashley, near Box in Wiltshire. When he is sure they are settled, he returns to Bath, where he is taken ill as a result of opium addiction, at the Greyhound Hotel. He is attended by Dr Parry, father of Charles Parry, one of his friends from Göttingen days. He cannot deliver the second set of lectures he had planned and they are postponed until the following year.
 19   STC writes a confessional letter to the Reverend Thomas Roberts ('the most eloquent preacher, I ever heard'), a Baptist minister in Bristol: 'O God save me – save me from myself . . . '.
(end)   He is back in Bristol with Wade, but visits the Morgan sisters when he can.

1814

January

STC is ill for much of the first half of the year and his lectures have to be postponed again. He seems to divide his time between Josiah Wade's in Bristol and the Morgans' at Ashley. Mrs C complains that she has had only one letter during an absence of two years.

April

2 (Sat) *Felix Farley's Bristol Journal* carries an announcement that STC is now recovered from a 'severe and protracted illness' and will give the six postponed lectures on Tuesday and Thursday evenings, on Milton and on *Don Quixote*. [This course is given in full, at the White Lion, on 5, 7, 12, 14, 19 and 21 of this month – although STC complains of an erysipelas condition which almost prevents him from completing the course.]

8 WW writes to Tom Poole asking him to see STC about Hartley's future. A fund must be raised for his university education. Lady Beaumont has offered £30 p.a.

17 and 18 RS replies to an offer from Cottle to raise a subscription for an annuity for STC, vigorously opposing the plan, talking of STC's 'most culpable habits of sloth and self-indulgence' and of the 'one accursed cause – excess in opium'. [Cottle as a result withdraws the idea.]

26 Moved by RS's letters, Cottle writes scathingly to STC, saying that he should renounce opium and return at once to Keswick. STC replies in anguish: 'I have prayed with drops of agony on my brow . . . I was seduced into the ACCURSED Habit ignorantly.'

STC plans two more sets of lectures, on the French Revolution and on female education. Only the first of the former series is given.

May

STC, although he is still unwell, writes long letters to Joseph Cottle and to John Prior Estlin on the nature of Christian belief, expounding the doctrine of the Trinity.

13 (Fri) STC writes to enquire after the health of Cottle, who is ill with a burst blood vessel.

14 STC writes to John Morgan (now reunited with his family in Ashley) that his opium sufferings have been like a descent into hell; he is now, he hopes, 'rising again, tho' slowly and gradu-

ally'. His will has not been his own. He speaks of 'wasted Talents'; of 'ingratitude to so many friends'; and of 'barbarous neglect of my family'. Josiah Wade has been helping him reduce the opium dosage by employing a man to sleep by his bed and supervise him during his cravings: 'Good God! Why do such good men love me!'

During May and June STC dines several times with an old Bristol friend, William Hood, and talks of Devonshire matters, goes to the theatre to see Charles Mathews in *Who Wants a Guinea?* and writes to Sir George Beaumont. Thanks to Hood's kindness, a Bristol physician, Henry Daniel, attends him.

June

10 (Fri) Washington Allston, after a long silence, visits STC, but there is, says STC, such 'a Levee in my bedroom that I had no opportunity of talking to him'. [During this year, Allston paints STC's portrait.]

11 STC writes to Morgan that he cannot travel to Ashley because of a return of the erysipelas condition.

26 He writes a letter of gratitude to Josiah Wade – 'I am unworthy to call any good man friend'; he hopes his plight may at least be a warning to others.

29 He reports himself to Morgan as greatly improved.

August

1 (Mon) *Remorse* is produced in Bristol. STC writes to John Murray the publisher, offering to translate *Faust*. [Later he gives up the idea after a humiliatingly low offer from Murray.]

27 STC's first reference, in an article in *Felix Farley's Bristol Journal*, to a proposed work on the Logos, 'the communicative intelligence in nature and in man'. Three articles by him appear in this journal during August and September, including 'On the Principles of Genial Criticism'.

September

12 (Mon) STC, now convalescent, joins the Morgans in lodgings at Ashley. He plans a large work on Christianity, the one true philosophy, comprising five treatises. He writes to Stuart, offering to contribute to the *Courier* again.

20 STC's series of 'Letters to Mr Justice Fletcher', dealing with affairs in Ireland, appear in the *Courier* (until 10 December).

October
STC walks with the Morgans to Corsham House to see the art collection of Paul Cobb Methuen. He is invited to stay a few days, and meets the Marquis of Lansdowne, who invites him to his house at Bowood.

December
STC moves with the Morgans to the house of a surgeon named Page at Calne in Wiltshire. [Here he stays for about a year.]

1815

January
2 (Mon) Mrs C writes to Poole about Hartley's future: RS has persuaded STC's brother George to allow Hartley £40 p.a.; Lady Beaumont will contribute £30 p.a. and Poole himself has offered £10 p.a. STC's nephew, William Hart Coleridge, has arranged a postmastership at Merton College, Oxford, for Hartley, worth £50 p.a.

March
7 (Tues) STC writes to Cottle, and again on 10th, offering work for publication, including the reissuing of the *Friend*, and asking for an advance of £30 or £40; he says he intends to move to Bristol and set up a school of about twenty pupils. Cottle sends only £5 and another £5 on receipt of the second letter. STC never writes to him again.
13 WW writes to ask Poole for the £10 promised to Hartley. If more money is required, he and RS will provide it. Southey and he have advised Hartley to work hard and gain independence.
26 STC at William Lisle Bowles's home at Bremhill, Wiltshire, correcting Bowles's poems. [He later says that Bowles 'took the corrections, but never forgave the corrector'.]
During this time STC is enjoying considerable social life at Calne. He has dined with the Marquis of Lansdowne (see November 1814) and has much conversation with Dr R. H. Brabant of Devizes. He becomes involved in local politics, giving a speech in Calne marketplace against the Corn Bill. He also argues against the peace treaty

with America (signed December 1814). William Hood, J. M. Gutch (STC's old schoolfellow from Christ's Hospital) and other friends join together to lend STC £45 to help him publish two volumes of his poetry. [This is *Sibylline Leaves*, published in 1817.]

April
3 (Mon) STC asks Lady Beaumont for a copy of his poem 'To William Wordsworth'. He comments on 'The Excursion' that, though full of beauties, it contains doctrines which are important to WW but 'come almost as Truisms or Commonplaces to Others'. [Lady B does not send the poem, but shows the letter to WW.]
(mid) STC writes to Lord Byron for help in finding a London publisher (preferably not Longman or Murray). [Byron agrees to help and suggests too that STC write a tragedy for London production.] STC is very troubled by Napoleon's continued power: 'These are awful times.'

May
6 (Sat) Hartley matriculates at Merton College, Oxford; he later spends part of his summer vacation with his father at Calne, where they see *Remorse* produced by a travelling company.
17 STC is worried because smallpox has appeared in Calne, and Charlotte Brent has never had it. He asks Dr Brabant for a vaccine.
22 WW has heard via Lady Beaumont that STC intends to publish his lines 'To William Wordsworth' (written 7 January 1807); he writes to say that the commendation, he feels, would be prejudicial to both of them, as *The Prelude* is not yet published.
25 STC tells Samuel Rogers that, if he were exiled, he would pass his summers in Zurich and the rest of the year alternately in Rome or Florence.
30 STC replies non-committally but affectionately to WW's letter, discussing the plan he had envisaged for 'The Excursion' and 'The Recluse'. He had hoped that one of WW's aims would be to explode the 'absurd notion . . . of Man's having progressed from an Ouran Outang state – so contrary to all History, to all Religion'. [He does eventually publish the WW poem in *Sibylline Leaves* as 'To a Gentleman'.]

From May to July STC develops his ideas about 'The Excursion' into a long preface to the *Poems*. [This is eventually to merge into the *Biographia Literaria*.] He dictates his ideas to John Morgan.

July

STC writes wryly to Dr Sainsbury of his desire to 'have himself opened before his own eyes' to find proof that his bodily ailments predated his addiction to opium. [An autopsy is held, as he had requested, after his death in 1834 and proof is found that his troubles were due to an enlarged heart.]

29 (Sat) STC writes to Brabant of the genesis of an 'Autobiographia Literaria', in which he is distancing himself from WW's poetical theory. This has developed from a mere preface to the *Poems* (March) into a work in its own right.

31 He dines with the Marquis and Marchioness of Lansdowne.

August

10 (Thurs) Morgan sends William Hood '57 sides of Coleridge's work'. He says proudly that 'C. can not work without me.'

September

STC writes to John M. Gutch about his intentions for the *BL*. Instead of poems and a preface, he plans to publish 'Biographical Sketches of my Literary Life' and 'Sibylline Leaves' (the latter to contain all his poems except for the unfinished 'Christabel'). He is writing a tragedy for Drury Lane at Christmas. [This is later abandoned because of 'the wretched state of my body and my mind'.] During this month a copy of the *Biographia Literaria* and of a volume of poems is sent to Bristol to be printed for Hood and Gutch by John Evans and Co. Mrs C writes to Poole that a Mr Kenyon has contributed £20 p.a. for five years to 'Mr Coleridge's other son'. [This is J. H. Kenyon, a Wiltshire friend.] STC visits Martha Fricker, his favourite of the Fricker sisters, now a mantua-maker in London, who is ill and has asked for him.

October

7 (Sat) STC gives Daniel Stuart a detailed account of his publishing plans: he is preparing three plays, *Richard II*, a rewritten version of Beaumont and Fletcher's *Pilgrim*, and another of their *Beggar's Bush*. (Someone, he says, has heard of his plans and has already brought out two of these plays.) He is also

working on a tragedy and on a 'Dramatic Entertainment' [*Zapolya*]. Most importantly, he has begun 'the Work on which I would wish to ground my reputation with Posterity', the Logosophia, in six treatises. He hopes desperately for patronage to complete this work.

13 Josiah Wade and his son, Lancelot, have offered to transcribe *BL* for an American edition.

15 STC sends *BL* to Lord Byron for comments. [Byron replies with compliments about 'Christabel', which Scott had read to him.]

22 STC tells Byron that 'Christabel' will be completed in five books and may be published with 'The Wanderings of Cain', 'of which I have, unfortunately, lost the only copy'.

25 STC writes to comfort Allston on the death of his wife. (She died in February 1815.)

28 Byron writes to Tom Moore to ask him to review STC's work favourably in the *Edinburgh Review*: STC only needs encouragement 'to explode most gloriously', he says.

November
During this month the first proofs of *Sibylline Leaves* are sent from Bristol.
(early) STC is laid low by 'a sudden and alarming illness' which lasts until the beginning of December.

4 (Sat) Byron sends a copy of 'Christabel' to John Murray, urging him to publish it.

December
(early) When STC recovers, he gives up the idea of writing a tragedy and instead completes the 'Dramatic Entertainment', now called *Zapolya*.
(late) He writes to Brabant of his opium dependence – 'this most pitiable Slavery'. He orders from a local chemist (Mr Kirkland) '3 ozs. laudanum ½ an oz of crude opium and 2 ozs of Tincture of Cardamum'.

1816

January

During this month STC corrects proofs of *Sibylline Leaves*, sent by John Evans, the Bristol printer, on behalf of J. M. Gutch the publisher.

7   (Sun) STC writes to a young friend from Calne, John Merewether, in praise of Merewether's mother: 'I have more than once wished to be 5 and 20 years younger, that I might only be able to fancy her my Mother.'

31   He tells Sotheby that the 'Dramatic Romance' (*Zapolya*) is nearly finished. He refers to *BL*, anticipating that neither WW nor WW's detractors will be satisfied with it; however, he feels that it is the 'true Philosophic Critique' which was needed and will be 'of more service to his just reputation than 20 idolators of his mannerisms'.

February

14   (Wed) The Literary Fund, at the instigation of Sotheby, gives STC a grant of £30.

15   Byron, though himself in financial difficulties, sends STC a present of £100.

March

(mid) STC comes up to London with John Morgan, to prepare *Zapolya* for production at Covent Garden. He takes up lodgings, reports Lamb, at the worst possible place for his addiction, a chemist's laboratory in Norfolk Street. STC collapses three days after his arrival and is only saved by a new physician, Dr Joseph Adams, an old acquaintance of Morgan's, who makes him stop the huge opium doses.

April

9   (Tues) *Zapolya* has been rejected by Covent Garden.

10   STC meets Byron and recites 'Kubla Khan' to him. [Byron is to leave England for good on 25 April.] Byron submits *Zapolya* to Drury Lane on STC's behalf, but it is soon rejected there too.

12   Arrangements are made for the publication of 'Christabel': at Byron's instigation, John Murray offers STC £80. Because of the Morgans' immediate need, STC accepts. Adams decides that STC should place himself under medical supervision and

recommends him to Dr James Gillman, in practice at Moreton House on Highgate Hill.

15   (Sat) STC arrives at Gillman's 'carrying the proofsheets of Christabel', Gillman later records. [He is to stay with the Gillmans for the rest of his life.] STC is not to be allowed out of the house to get opium, but within eight days he has found a way of acquiring the drug without Gillman's knowledge. Morgan is to come every day from 11.30 a.m. until 3.15 p.m. to act as STC's amanuensis.

During this time STC develops a friendship with John Hookham Frere, diplomat and translator. He tells John Murray (8 May 1816) that he regards the day he met Frere as 'among the most memorable Red Letter Days of my Literary Life'.

May

8   (Wed) STC criticises Daniel Stuart and the *Courier* for its shift of political stance. It supports the reinstatement of the Duke of York (although it had previously published STC's article criticising the reinstatement). He offers him a tract, to be divided into a series of articles, on the Catholic question.

13   STC invites Stuart to dinner at the Gillmans'.

25   'Kubla Khan', the fragment of 'Christabel' and 'The Pains of Sleep' are published by John Murray as an octavo pamphlet of 64 pages; they receive unfavourable reviews. [However, the volume is reprinted twice during the year.]

June

2   (Sun) The *Examiner* publishes a scathing review of 'Christabel' by William Hazlitt.

6   STC signs an agreement with Murray over the 'Christmas Tale' (*Zapolya*): he will receive £50 for an edition of 1000 copies.

July

8   (Mon) Murray has been discouraged by the poor reception of 'Christabel'. STC negotiates with Gale and Fenner (formerly Gale and Curtis) who had reprinted the *Friend* in 1812. He prepares *Lay Sermons* for them.

14   He is visited by CL and HCR, from whom he borrows books (he complains that people unjustly accuse him of losing them!). Gillman dismisses the visitors shortly after their arrival:

'Gentlemen, it is time for you to go!' CL says he will never call again [though he does, after a gap, and eventually becomes reconciled to Gillman].

19 STC is invited by J. H. Frere to meet George Canning.

(mid) Gutch sends proofs of *BL*, expecting STC to add 150 pages to complete the second volume.

August
29 (Thurs) An article appears in the *Courier* attacking the management of Drury Lane Theatre for putting on C. R. Maturin's *Bertram*. It is by STC with help, probably only as amanuensis, from John Morgan. [Further criticism by STC appears on 7, 9, 10 and 11 September and all are reprinted in *BL*, ch. xxiii, causing a rift with Byron.]

31 (Sat) STC tells Thomas Boosey, the bookseller, that he plans a fortnightly or monthly letter on German literature. He borrows German reference books from Boosey.

September
18 (Wed) STC goes with the Gillmans to the seaside at Muddiford in Hampshire.

In the autumn Derwent leaves school and becomes a private tutor in Lancashire, hoping for an opportunity to go to university. Mrs C is delighted that, at the Gillmans, STC has resumed regular contact with his family by letter, having written scarcely at all for the previous three years.

December
The Statesman's Manual published. Hazlitt attacks it in the *Edinburgh Review*, continuing the campaign against STC he began in June. First *Lay Sermons* volume published by Gale and Fenner.

18 Gutch sends in his printing bill for *BL* – £284. STC turns for help to Gale and Fenner. (Gutch has delayed sending in the bill because of William Hood's intervention.)

21 (Sat) HCR and his friend Cargill visit STC at Highgate and spend 1½ hours with him. STC looks ill, says he has bowel trouble. Gillman, however, says STC drinks only three glasses of wine a day and only takes opium when prescribed by Gillman himself. STC is working on the second and third *Lay Sermons* and *Poems and Memoirs*. He explains his idea of Fancy as 'memory without judgement'. He mentions Hazlitt's attack on him calmly.

1817

January

STC speaks of unknown enemies working against him; there are disputes with Gutch, who may have been affected by the malicious interference of Thomas Curtis (still very much involved in the running of Gale and Fenner). [Gutch criticises STC in letters to CL, another old schoolfriend of his.]

14 (Tues) Gale and Fenner are negotiating with Gutch and ask him to 'state the amount of Advances to Mr Coleridge on the "Literary Life &c." and the printing Charges'.

February

6 (Thurs) STC writes gratefully to Josiah Wedgwood and agrees to transfer to Mrs C the right to draw the £75 p.a. left to him by Thomas Wedgwood.

The manuscript of *BL* is longer than one volume but not long enough for two (see July 1816); STC therefore reclaims the manuscript of *Zapolya* from John Murray (who had paid £59 for individual publishing rights) to fill the gap. Although in the end he does not use the play, substituting *Satyrane's Letters* instead, there is a break with Murray, who is misled by Thomas Curtis (acting for Gale and Fenner) into thinking STC is guilty of double-dealing. After this dispute, STC has his works published by Gale and Fenner (soon to become Rest Fenner), of Paternoster Row, rather than by Murray.

March

14 (Fri) STC vetoes the separate publication by Gale and Fenner (now Rest Fenner) of *Zapolya*, declaring that this would be a betrayal of his agreement with Murray [but see November 1817].

26 He pays Murray £50 to reclaim *Zapolya*.

April

During this month the second volume of *Lay Sermons* is published.

7 (Mon) STC discusses with Rest Fenner the publishing of an *Encyclopaedia Metropolitana* – a 'History of Human Knowledge'.

(late) STC visits Martha Fricker and from there writes to arrange to meet RS on his visit to London.

May

13   (Tues) Rest Fenner have sorted out the sheets of the *Poems*,
     sent to them in disarray by J. M. Gutch. This costs them £28.

June

13   (Fri) STC has a 'MOST DELIGHTFUL Evening' with the German
     writer, Ludvig Tieck (whom he had met in Rome), at the home
     of J. H. Green, the surgeon, soon to become one of STC's
     closest friends and followers.

18   STC asks for a £300 advance if he is to accept the job of editor
     of the *Encyclopaedia Metropolitana*.

21   Curtis replies on behalf of Rest Fenner that the money for the
     editorship will only be forthcoming if STC leaves Highgate
     and lives at Camberwell [where he can be supervised by
     Curtis's brother, Samuel].

24 and 25   Ludvig Tieck stays with STC at Highgate and the latter's
     admiration for him grows. ('His literary Career bears a strik-
     ing resemblance to Wordsworth's', he writes to J. H. Frere.)

July

Biographia Literaria and *Sibylline Leaves* are both published by Rest
Fenner. STC has refused to leave Highgate and has therefore had to
withdraw from the editorship of the *Encyclopaedia Metropolitana*
[though he does eventually contribute a *Treatise on Method*]. Gillman
lowers his charges to help STC. WW is offended by STC's comments
on his work (see December 1817). Byron is also offended at STC's
attack on Drury Lane. Although he continues to admire 'Christabel',
he writes of STC, 'he is a shabby fellow and I wash my hands of and
after him'. Hartley is with his father during this month. He is befriended by his cousins (sons of James and George) and wishes to
visit the West Country. STC is glad to see the family rift being healed
in the next generation. STC meets Poole on his visit to London late in
the month.

August

14   (Thurs) RS visits STC, reluctantly [afraid STC intends to re-
     turn to Keswick].

18   STC signs a contract with Rest Fenner allowing them after all
     to publish *Zapolya* separately. [This is the result of his financial
     difficulties.]

23   (Sat) Hartley leaves Highgate for Nether Stowey.

September
STC is at the seaside for his health – at Littlehampton in Sussex. From there he writes a placatory letter to Murray, hoping to heal the rift. On the beach during this month he meets and makes friends with H. F. Cary, the translator of Dante. During the autumn Derwent, without telling his father, accepts a post as a tutor with the Hopwoods in Lancashire, while he waits for funds to go to Cambridge.

October
STC spends the month at Littlehampton. This month's edition of *Blackwood's Magazine* includes a scathing review of *BL*, probably by John Wilson, which attacks not only the book but the author, and revives the charge that he has deserted his wife and children. [STC asks HCR and WW for advice on taking libel action: both consider this inadvisable and the matter is dropped.]

November
13   (Tues) STC returns to Highgate.
During this month *Zapolya* is published by Rest Fenner. Tieck visits Highgate.

December
11   (Thurs) STC gives a lecture to the London Philosophical Society on the principles of experimental philosophy.
23   STC is hoping to organise an Anglo-German Society. (He has already written to J. H. Frere about this.)
27   WW dines with Tom Monkhouse in Queen Street where he meets STC. HCR, also present, feels STC emerges to advantage: he is respectful, WW cold and scornful (probably because of STC's comments on his work in *BL*). HCR hears STC quoting WW's verse – and WW also quoting WW's verse!
30   STC and WW are both at a large dinner-party at the Lambs'. HCR notes that 'two parties congregate around the two poets – but STC's is larger than WW's'.
During this year STC has published *A Hebrew Dirge* (a translation of Hyman Hurwitz's funeral offering to Princess Charlotte).

1818

January

During this month the *Treatise on Method* is published in the *Encyclopaedia Metropolitana*.

8 (Thurs) STC writes to Derwent about his eagerness to save enough money to send him to Cambridge, although 'I know not in what respect I can lessen my expenses'. He hopes money will be available in a year's time. Hartley is with his father at Highgate before returning to Merton College, Oxford, on 17th.

16 STC writes admiringly to his nephew, William Hart Coleridge [later Bishop of Barbados], praising him for his manner of conducting a baptism. He regrets his own decision not to enter Holy Orders: 'I suffered myself to be seduced from a path of Duty laid down for me, and in which alone I was qualified to have been truly useful.'

27 STC begins a series of fourteen lectures for the London Philosophical Society. They are on Tuesday and Friday evenings and deal with literature from the Middle Ages to the Restoration. [They are to be financially his most successful.] Through them he gains another disciple, Thomas Allsop, who later is to call himself STC's 'favourite disciple'.

30 STC, who has learnt at last of the machinations of Thomas Curtis over his publishing arrangements, now talks of the 'baseness and profligate dishonesty' of Rest Fenner (he calls them 'Curtis and Fenner'). He is now negotiating with 'one of the most respectable Houses in London', Taylor and Hessey of Fleet Street. Second lecture for London Philosophical Society.

February

STC's lectures continue on 3, 6, 10, 13, 17, 20, 24 and 27 of this month.

2 (Mon) STC has received a 'handsome, friendly Letter' from Taylor and Hessey, offering to publish his works.

6 He is reading and studying Blake's *Songs of Innocence and Experience*.

24 (Tues) HCR takes a Mrs Smith to STC's lecture on 'Wit and Humour'; he comments that there was much obscurity and metaphysics in it.

April
1   (Wed) Hartley is still at Highgate. He 'improves perceptibly', says STC, attributing this largely to Mrs Gillman's influence.
3   STC dines with William Hart Coleridge.
30 He writes a pamphlet in defence of Sir Robert Peel's Bill for regulating the labour of children in the cotton factories. [The Bill passes the House of Commons but is held up in the Lords. STC produces two pamphlets in all, and is instrumental in the eventual passing of the Bill.]

May
3   (Sun) STC is still working for the cause of the 'cotton-children' and writes to find out from HCR if there is already a law regulating their employment.
(early) He sleeps away from home for 'the first time in more than two years' as he continues to campaign for the Child Labour Bill.
26 He gives a supernumary lecture to cover material he has not found time for during the series.
He plans six lectures on Shakespeare this month, but later abandons the idea.

June
This summer Thomas Phillips paints STC's portrait.
13 (Sat) STC leaves Highgate to stay for eight days with J. H. Green at the latter's mother's house in Malden. The reason is '[p]artly from the state of my health . . . and partly from other causes'. The two men work hard at STC's writings. Some time this year, Green undertakes to take over the payment of STC's insurance premiums.

November
4   (Wed) STC is shown William Collins's portrait of daughter Sara and is delighted.
A three-volume edition of the *Friend* is published, largely made up of the original 1809–10 material but including three new essays on morals and religion as well as a corrected version of his *Treatise on Method*, which had appeared in mangled form in the *Encyclopaedia Metropolitana* in January 1818. C. R. Leslie paints STC's portrait.

December
STC delivers a course of fourteen lectures on the history of philoso-

phy and another course of six lectures on Shakespeare, at the 'Crown and Anchor' in the Strand. The dates of the first course are: 14 and 28 December 1818; in 1819: 4, 11, 18 and 25 January, 8, 15, 22 February and 1, 8, 15, 22 and 29 March. The dates of the second course are: 17 and 31 December 1818, and 7, 14, 21 and 28 January 1819. Some time during this year STC meets Sara H in London on her way to the Clarksons. He also meets his brother James in London.

1819

January
STC continues with the two lecture courses at the 'Crown and An-chor' (for full dates, see entry for December 1818).
8 (Fri) He writes at length to a young correspondent about the choice of a marriage partner and relations between the sexes. Hartley is again with his father before returning to Oxford in the middle of the month.

February
STC talks of lecturing at the Russell Institute, but nothing comes of the idea.

March
During this month, Rest Fenner become bankrupt. False returns have been made and STC cheated out of his rightful profits. (He estimates his loss at over £1000). In an effort to make money he even has interviews with *Blackwood's*, which had pilloried him over *BL* (possibly the writer was John Wilson, WW's friend, with whom STC may have quarrelled at Allan Bank). However, no agreement is reached. [Only two pieces by STC, probably not sent in by him, appear in *Blackwood's* during 1819.]

April
11 (Sun) STC meets John Keats-by chance, while walking with Green down Millfield Lane in Highgate; Green had been Keats's demonstrator at Guy's Hospital. STC later recalls Keats as 'a loose, slack, not well-dressed youth'; Keats writes more enthu-

siastically that they walked two miles together and that 'in those two Miles he broached a thousand things'.

14   Hartley is elected Probationary Fellow of Oriel College, Oxford.

During this month STC suffers badly from influenza.

May
6   (Thurs) STC writes to introduce himself, as 'Your old and sincere Admirer', to his new neighbour, the famous comic actor, Charles Mathews.

June
STC again visits J. H. Green's mother at St Lawrence, near Maldon in Essex, but does not enjoy himself without the Gillmans.

August
He is on holiday with the Gillmans at Ramsgate.

September
4   (Sat) He writes coldly to Byron, who has, in *Don Juan*, accused him of drunkenness. [Byron's opinion of STC has changed since the publication of *BL* and since he heard rumours that RS and STC were accusing Shelley and himself of incest.]

STC is eager to send Derwent to Cambridge, but his job as a tutor means that he cannot go up until October 1820.

October
8   (Fri) STC receives a gift of £100 from Thomas Allsop, who has heard of the bankruptcy of Rest Fenner.

Hartley takes up his Fellowship at Oriel College, Oxford. [This is not a success as he drinks and smokes heavily and cannot live up to the rigorous standard of behaviour expected of the Fellows; see May 1820.]

November
Pressure is being put on STC to contribute regularly to *Blackwood's Magazine*. John Morgan suffers a severe stroke. STC stays with the family and hopes for his recovery. [Morgan is again in severe financial trouble. By the end of the year he is probably in prison for debt and in 1820 he dies.]

1820

January
CL and Mary L pay their New Year visit. During this year Gillman allows STC to spend some time in Town; he can dine occasionally with Sir George Beaumont, Basil Montagu (with whom he is again on good terms), Daniel Stuart, Thomas Monkhouse, John Hookham Frere and Joseph Henry Green. He is in correspondence with Hyman Hurwitz and C. A. Tulk about religion, and with James Gooden about Kant.

March
9   (Thurs) Death of Hartley's beloved Mrs Wilson of Greta Hall at the age of 77. She leaves £20 for H and £5 each to Derwent and Sara.
30   (Thurs) STC tells Thomas Allsop of his plans for the following works:
   (a) 'Characteristics of Shakespeare's Dramatic Works';
   (b) 'Philosophical Analysis of the Genius and Works of Dante';
   (c) 'The History of Philosophy' in two volumes (from his 1818–19 lectures);
   (d) 'Letters on the Old and New Testament'.
He also hopes to finish 'Christabel' and to write an epic poem on the destruction of Jerusalem.

April
8   (Sat) Hartley and Derwent are at Highgate. STC is delighted by their affection for each other, their high spirits and their 'manly independence of intellect'. He is hoping to send Derwent to Cambridge (see 7 October 1820).

May
HNC stays overnight at Highgate to make Derwent's acquaintance. STC is unwell and believes it is 'a summons. God's Will be done!'
24   (Wed) Thomas Allsop stays and 'behaves more like a dutiful son than an Acquaintance'. STC sees RS, who is in London, and sends north with him a book for 'little Sara'. The College decides to deprive Hartley of his Oriel Fellowship (STC hears of the decision in the following month).

June
Tom Poole is at Highgate. Together he and Derwent visit Richard
Sharp MP.
17   (Sat) STC is introduced by J. H. Frere to Lord Liverpool and
dines with him, Canning and other public figures.
The WWs and DW are in London this month, but STC cannot dine
with them at Thomas Monkhouse's because of a prior engagement.
During this month STC is visited by the Swedenborgian James
Arbouin: C. A. Tulk has suggested that STC will write a history of
the mind of Swedenborg. However, during the visit STC proves less
than committed to the ideas of Swedenborg and the project is
dropped. News reaches STC of Hartley's loss of his Fellowship
because of 'sottishness, a love of low company and general inatten-
tion to college rules'. Derwent, who is visiting his father, later says
(in his *Memoir* of Hartley): 'I never have seen any human being,
before or since, so deeply affected.' This marks the beginning of
what STC calls one of the four 'griping and grasping Sorrows' of his
life.

July
STC hears from Derwent, who has gone to Oxford after his brother,
that Hartley has left and is probably in Birmingham.

August
8   (Tues) STC writes to Allsop that he has settled Hartley for six
to eight weeks with the Montagus. He and Hartley are at work
on an essay on metre and rhythm in Greek and English verse,
using John Hookham Frere's new translations of Aristophanes.
He criticises WW's poetry because of its 'Nature worship'
which is dependent on 'accidents of Birthplace and Abode'.
He is reading Dobrizhoffer's account of the Abipones [later to
be translated by Sara Coleridge].
J. H. Green comes every week to record STC's work on the Old &
New Testaments.

September
21   (Thurs) Derwent, reports STC in a letter to Allsop, is staying
at Charles Lloyd's near Kensington.
26   In a letter to Mary Evans (now Mrs Fryer Todd), STC reports
that Derwent will leave him in a few days to go to Cambridge,
while he himself will go to Oxford to speak to Edward

Copleston, Provost of Oriel, on behalf of Hartley. He is discouraging about Mrs Todd's idea of setting up a school, and sad that he cannot help her financially himself.

October

7 (Sat) Thanks to the generosity of J. H. Frere and others, Derwent goes to St John's College, Cambridge. Poole has tried in vain to get him an Exhibition there; however, he is soon elected to a Foundress Scholarship at the College.

11 In a letter to Allsop, STC expresses strong sympathy for Queen Caroline. (The Bill to deprive her of her title is now being debated in the Lords.)

14 STC arrives in Oxford. Before the interview with Copleston he reads and annotates a copy of John Petvin's *Letters Concerning Mind* (1750).

15 STC has an interview with Copleston: he tries to explain Hartley's natural eccentricity, which he believes has turned the College authorities against him;

17 Despite STC's intervention, the Fellows of Oriel College at their statutable meeting ratify their decision to deprive Hartley of his Fellowship and agree to pay him £300 compensation or, as Hartley puts it, to 'let matters be hushed up'. STC encourages H to refuse the offer but he later accepts it (see 15 January 1822).

November

STC unwell. He keeps Hartley busy sending explanatory letters to those who had financed him during his undergraduate years at Merton: Lady Beaumont, Poole and his uncle George at Ottery. STC is still trying to complete his work on Logic [he never does] and an 'Assertion of Religion'.

December

8 (Fri) STC meets HCR, who reports him as 'looking well'. He composes a letter for Hartley to send to the Warden of Merton College in an attempt to clear his name.

STC is involved in the quarrel between J. G. Lockhart of *Blackwood's Magazine*, and John Scott, editor of the *London Magazine*. Lockhart had published a private letter of STC's in *Blackwood's*; Scott had attacked this, speaking (without warrant) of STC's displeasure (see February 1821).

1821

February

Duel between J. G. Lockhart and John Scott – Scott killed. Thereafter STC addresses his communications with *Blackwood's* to the publisher, W. Blackwood, not to Lockhart.

April

STC writes letters to C. A. Tulk MP on the Catholic question.

May

The Gillmans and STC entertain the Lambs, Mr and Mrs Charles Mathews and Allsop at Highgate.

16 (Mon) STC writes to Derwent at Cambridge warning him against scattering 'the stream of your Power and Time in a multiplicity of Channels'.

June

8 (Fri) George Coleridge is to visit STC during a stay in London, but does not keep the appointment.

11 STC writes affectionately to George of his disappointment at not seeing him. He writes of having been 'misinterpreted and misrepresented'. Derwent stays at Highgate, tries in vain to visit his uncle George and dines with his cousin, John Taylor Coleridge.

12 Mrs Montagu informs STC reluctantly that Hartley can no longer stay with them: he has taken to vanishing and giving no hint of his whereabouts. The Gillmans take Hartley in, as he is ill, and he later moves to the home of his one boyhood friend, Robert Jameson, from Ambleside, at 1 Gray's Inn Square, where he continues his habit of disappearing without warning for days at a time.

(late) Allsop's sister visits STC. Later he writes at length to advise 'a Young Lady' (possibly Miss Allsop) about marriage. [He is often called upon for advice by young admirers of both sexes. Five such letters are extant.]

July

STC writes to Poole for the 'two Autobiographical Letters' he had sent him in Stowey days [actually there were five] and a copy of the letter from Germany describing the ascent of the Brocken.

August
STC writes to De Quincey of the 'unprecedented friendship' of the Gillmans. He is indebted to Mr Gillman for £500, but Gillman has struck off £120 as incurred for Hartley and Derwent, both of whom are in London during the summer. During the second half of the year Allsop becomes more reticent with STC, partly because of his marriage plans and partly because he is offended with Mrs Gillman, whom he feels to be unworthy of STC's enormous respect.

September
19 (Wed) STC sends a package of articles to *Blackwood's Magazine*, including 'The ideal of a Magazine', 'Witchcraft', 'Faeryland' and the 'Life of Holty', with specimens of his poems translated into English.

21 He supports the governors of Highgate Free Grammar School, who intend to petition Parliament to bring in a bill authorising them to pull down the school chapel and build a new one with funds drawn from the Highgate Charity. Some influential Highgate residents object that this would involve 'misuse' of the Charity's funds; STC rightly predicts that there will be a feud.

24 STC receives £50 from Allsop.

October
Sara Coleridge has translated an anthropological work, 'An Account of the Abipones, an Equestrian People of Paraguay', from the Latin of Martin Dobrizhoffer. She intended it as a contribution to Derwent's college fees, but these are now paid. [The book is published in three volumes in 1822.]

1 (Mon) STC to Ramsgate for the sea air, with the Gillmans and Mrs Gillman's sister. They stay at 7 Wellington Crescent, East Cliff. John Watson is now living with the Gillmans in Highgate as a 'temporary partner' of Mr Gillman. [He becomes one of STC's devoted helpers.] STC writes to advise Allsop on matrimony.

November
17 (Sat) All back to Highgate.
*c.*23 WW, on a visit to London, walks over to Highgate to see STC.

1822

January

11 (Fri) STC writes to Derwent at Cambridge, accusing him of wasting his time with social life and 'Coxcombry' – he seems to object even to D's being secretary of a literary club.

15 STC is displeased to hear that John Taylor Coleridge has accepted the £300 on Hartley's behalf from Oriel College. In response to a letter from Derwent, STC writes to him encouragingly to 'give your poor Brother an example, instead of an excuse'.

18 STC writes to John Murray, the publisher, with a proposal for a life of Archbishop Leighton. [Murray later declines this offer.]

25 STC writes to Allsop of his idea for a pupil scheme: he already effectively has two pupils, Charles Stutfield and John Watson.

February

25 (Mon) The *Courier* carries an advertisement from STC that he proposes to take select pupils 'not younger than 19 or 20, for the purpose of assisting them in the formation of their minds, and the regulation of their studies'. [This class does materialise.]

March

STC 'very unwell'. He continues to write to Allsop to help him adjust to his marriage, mentioning Mrs C and Sara H as a way of aiding him by example.

15 He writes in greater detail to Daniel Stuart about his plans to set up a class of young men, the course to last two years.

This spring, Sara Coleridge's translation of Dobrizhoffer is published (see Oct 1821).

May

STC writes to John Dawes, who runs a school in Ambleside, to arrange for Hartley to take up a teaching post there. RS and the WWs are not eager for him to return north however, and Hartley himself, faced with their opposition, begs for more time in London. STC's letter to Dawes contains a long justification of his own role as a father: since Hartley's visit to Calne, STC feels he has done his best for him. He describes H's character: 'of all the Waifs I ever knew,

Hartley is the least likely and the least calculated to lead any human being astray by his example'. He feels bitter about WW's intervention: WW has been writing directly to Gillman to ask him to dissuade H from coming north.

June
(late)   Derwent falls ill at Highgate with typhus fever and is nursed by the Gillmans.

July
Hartley too has been staying at Highgate. STC writes him a chiding letter suggesting that he should accept correction more readily and that he should take the school job. After reading this, Hartley vanishes again, in the middle of his brother's illness. STC sees this as desertion, and is deeply upset.

August
3   (Sat) STC writes to Allsop that Derwent is now out of danger and that he hopes that Hartley will soon set off for the north, despite the protests of his mother, who seems, he says, not to care what happens to her son as long as she is spared the 'occasional annoyance' or 'Mr Wordsworth's disapprobation'.

October
(early)   STC goes to Walmer with Mrs Gillman for a holiday, realising that he has 'no longer power to make better or worse' matters with Hartley. While he is away, H is persuaded, probably by Mr Gillman, to go north.
8   (Tues) STC writes to Allsop about his four 'griping and grasping Sorrows' – the impossibility of a happy marriage; the break with the WWs; the alienation from Sara Hutchinson; and the disappointments over his sons.
28   STC is now at Ramsgate, from where he writes to thank Gillman for his 'unweariable kindness' to Hartley.

November
(mid)   STC still at Ramsgate. He meets Lord Liverpool and George Canning.
19   (Tues) Hartley is now teaching at the Reverend Dawes's school in Ambleside. DW writes of him as 'the oddest creature imaginable, no taller than De Quincey, and with a raven-black beard'.

December
This month STC meets Thomas Moore, and Edward Irving makes his first visit to Highgate. Mrs Gillman and STC have a disagreement about the servants, leading STC to write her a long letter about his own social background as a 'poor, friendless Bluecoat Boy'.

21 (Sat) STC is at a party at Charles Aders'. HCR describes him as 'the star of the evening': he apparently talks deprecatingly about both WW and RS, reproaching the former for 'a vulgar attachment to orthodoxy'.

28 STC dines with J. T. Coleridge and meets Henry Nelson Coleridge again.

29 HNC records in *Table Talk* STC's discussion of the character of Othello, of Byron, Kemble and Mathews (presumably from the previous evening).

1823

January
1 (Tues) STC talks (*Table Talk*) of Parliamentary privilege, the permanency and progression of nations and Kant's distinction of three races of mankind.

3 Mrs C and daughter Sara visit Highgate for the first time.

4 STC talks of the importance of logic in this age, of Plato and Xenophon, of Greek drama, Kotzebue, Burke and plagiarists.

5 HNC visits Highgate with his brother John and meets Mrs C and Sara (see March.)

6 STC talks of St John's Gospel, the nature of Christianity, the Epistle to the Hebrews, the Logos and Reason and Understanding.

March
Mrs C and Sara leave for the north in the middle of the month, having gone on from Highgate at the end of January to visit John Taylor Coleridge and his wife in London. STC has been too ill to leave the house during their stay. Sara and HNC are secretly engaged. Sara H is in London. STC procures for her a seat for an oratorio, which she attends with John Monkhouse. 'We both of us had a comfortable nap', she records.

April

4 (Fri) Thomas Monkhouse gives a dinner at which STC, WW, Moore, Rogers and CL are present, as well as HCR, Gillman, Mary W and Sara H. 'I dined in Parnassus', writes CL, 'half the Poetry of England constellated and clustered in Gloster Place.' STC was 'in his finest vein of talk'. HCR notes of STC, 'WW he chiefly talked to.'

5 STC and WW attend a musical party at Charles Aders'.

27 STC talks of Kean, of Sir James Mackintosh, Sir Humphrey Davy, Robert Smith, Canning, the National Debt and the Poor Laws.

28 He talks of the inconsistent conduct of the Whigs and of the movement for reform in the House of Commons.

29 He talks of the Church of Rome saying that 'we' (the Church of England) are the real Catholics.

30 He talks of the Zendusta (the sacred book of Zoroastra) and of pantheism and idolatry.

May

1 (Thurs) STC talks of the difference between stories of dreams and ghosts, and tells the anecdote of the phantom portrait (later used by Washington Irving in his *Tales of a Traveller*), of the Witch of Endor and of Socinianism.

June

5 (Thurs) STC asks John Taylor Coleridge to read over his work on logic and, if he approves, to speak to John Murray, the publisher, about it.

12 STC himself sees Murray about publishing the logic book and Murray agrees to be his publisher. (However, it proves impossible to see Murray a second time.) Derwent visits his father for a day on his way to Eton – in a 'very unsettled state of mind', says STC.

July

STC still in touch with Mrs Morgan and her sister, Miss Brent. He asks the latter to send him RS's *Brazil*.

23 He gives detailed route instructions to his nephew Edward for his forthcoming visit to Keswick.

August
John Murray proves very distant in relations with STC and lays down severe stipulations about publishing the *Poems*, insisting that he accept H. H. Milman as editor.

8 (Fri) STC sends the *Life of Leighton* to the publishers Taylor and Hessey and they accept it.

14 He tells C. A. Tulk that he will send his own selection of poems to Murray and hopes they will be accepted.

15 He and Tulk decide to stop negotiations with Murray.

He writes to Taylor and Hessey about their decision to publish his *Aids to Reflection*. They are also to publish his *Elements of Discourse* and *The Assertion of Religion*. STC writes fatherly letters of advice to James Gillman Junior (aged 15).

October
11 (Sat) STC to Ramsgate.

18 STC writes to Sara H that he will be delighted to dine and spend the evening with her and the Monkhouses. (Mrs Tom Monkhouse has come to Ramsgate for her health; Sara H is staying with her and says she is bored.)

November
STC spends the early part of the month at Ramsgate, calling on Sara H two or more times and working on the proofs of the *Aids to Reflection*. During his absence the Gillmans move from Moreton House to 3 The Grove, Highgate. STC chooses an attic room as his 'Bed and Bookroom'.

11 (Tues) He refuses an invitation to lecture to the Literary and Philosophical Society in Leeds because of his health.

December
10 (Wed) STC writes to Allsop that Mrs Gillman has had a bad fall and broken her arm. He invites Allsop to spend Christmas Day with them, but Mrs Allsop complains that it is the season for *family* reunions.

1824

January

18 (Mon) STC visits CL, who has been ill for several weeks.

24 Derwent is granted a pass degree at Cambridge. He is now, says his father, 'an avowed Atheist' – influenced, STC thinks, by his friends T. B. Macaulay and Charles Austin. He refuses to read for Honours or to take Holy Orders, but becomes third master at Plymouth School.

February

STC declines an offer from the London Institute to lecture, because of his health and distance from Town.

March

10 (Wed) STC writes to Thomas H. Dunn (Highgate chemist) about his payment of a bill for opium: 'I intreat you, be careful not to have any note delivered to me unless I am alone and passing your door.'

16 STC is elected, largely through the efforts of Montagu, as a Royal Associate of the newly founded Royal Society of Literature and receives an annual grant of 100 guineas. He has to deliver an annual essay (see 18 May 1825).

(late) STC spends about ten days with the Allsops (possibly after a slight coolness with Mrs Gillman, who makes him feel 'fidget-watched').

April

3 (Sat) STC dines at the Monkhouses in Gloucester Place. It is probably here that he meets WW and receives WW's translation of the first three books of the *Aeneid*.

7 (Wed) After receiving a conciliatory note from Mrs Gillman, STC is 'fetched home' by Gillman this evening.

19 STC writes affectionately to his nephew John Taylor Coleridge, speaking of the suppression of 'the affections of consanguinity' in himself because of the circumstances of his life and character. He is therefore even more pleased to be so fond of John and his wife. He speaks of his own poor health for the past two or three months and the equally poor health of the Gillmans.

From now until the end of his life, STC devotes himself to what he thinks of as his greatest task: a defence of Trinitarian Christianity. He therefore works this year at *Aids to Reflection*, which reaches the proof stage in March 1825.

May

6 (Thurs) STC is formally presented to the Royal Society of Literature. HNC comes to Highgate during this month and April and continues to record his uncle's conversation (later published as *Table Talk*.)

8 STC talks to HNC of Plato and Xenophon, of the religion of the Greeks, of Egyptian antiquities and of Milton and Virgil.

25 STC suggests Thursday as the best day for the author, Henry Taylor, to visit. Thus the Thursday evening meetings are gradually established.

June

2 (Wed) STC criticises Granville Penn's book against Professor Buckland: Penn supports the notion of the Deluge. STC says: 'Science will be superceded, if every phenomenon is to be referred in this manner to an actual miracle.'

5 STC talks of English and Greek dancing and of Greek acoustics.

7 He talks of Lord Byron's versification and of Don Juan.

10 A large gathering at Highgate – HCR, CL, the Gillmans, the Aders, Henry Taylor, William Collins the painter, Basil Montagu, HNC and so on. 'A rich evening', says HCR. HNC records STC's comment that marriage between first cousins is possibly undesirable, but that he is prepared to waive his objections as it is countenanced by St Augustine and the Church.

During this month Thomas Carlyle and Gabriel Rossetti (father of D. G. and Christina) also visit Highgate.

October

6 (Wed) STC to Ramsgate.

14 STC dines at Sir Thomas Gray's.

24 DW writes that her nephew William attends Hartley's school in Ambleside; Hartley now has fourteen scholars and is, says his father, 'universally beloved'.

(autumn) STC writes to Thomas H. Dunn, the Highgate chemist, for 'an oz of the Liquor Morphii, equal in strength to Laudanum'; an apprentice of the firm, S. T. Porter, later writes that he was accustomed to fill STC's laudanum bottle 'every five or six days' and that STC seemed to need 'more than an ordinary wine-glassful a day'. STC spends October and most of November at Ramsgate, accompanied by Mrs Gillman, at 29 Wellington Crescent; they are visited by the Gillmans' sons James and Henry. STC gives the latter a grounding in Greek grammar. Sir Alexander and Lady Johnston (the latter 'not unlike Miss Sara Hutchinson in face and mouth') pay STC great attention.

November
23 (Tues) STC witnesses the wrecking of a skiff and a West Indiaman in a storm off Ramsgate Pier.

December
13 (Mon) STC writes a letter of introduction for Gabriel Rossetti to H. F. Cary. (GR has been exiled from Italy because of his writings.)

1825

January
24 (Mon) STC writes to the sculptor John Flaxman for help in preparing an essay on sculpture and religion.

February
STC writes a letter of introduction for Allsop to Sir Humphrey Davy as 'an old friend'.

March
15 (Tues) STC writes to C. A. Tulk apologising for not having contacted him since the death of Tulk's wife in October 1824. He had apparently written a long letter, then had a vision of Mrs Tulk, after which the letter seemed so inadequate that he destroyed it. The proofs of *Aids to Reflection* are ready for the press – to be published by Taylor and Hessey. The biography of Leighton has now become central to this work and is not to be published separately.

April

15 (Fri) Edward Coleridge, brother of John Taylor and Henry Nelson, brings his Italian friend Gioacchino de'Prati to Highgate. STC enlists Edward's patronage for Henry, the Gillman's younger son, so that he can be entered for Eton. (Edward is to take up a post there this month.) STC is still working to reclaim the money owed to Derwent for his two St John's College Exhibitions.

26 He writes to Richard Cattermole of the Royal Society of Literature with the title of 'the first specimen of a series of Disquisitions' on religion in Ancient Greece; he apologises for not having produced a lecture the previous year.

May

STC writes to DW ('an unusual event, a letter from Coleridge', she observes to Catherine Clarkson), to ask her to use her influence to help James Gillman Junior become medical attendant to Mr Harrison, 'the Quaker barrister', who is coming to live in Highgate.

7 (Sat) He writes to his publishers, Taylor and Hessey, with a list of forthcoming works:

(a) 'On Faith';
(b) 'On the Eucharist';
(c) 'On the Philosophy of Prayer';
(d) 'On the Hebrew Prophets';
(e) 'On the Church';
(f) 'On the Use of the Scriptures'.

[Only (e) is published in STC's lifetime, as 'On the Church and the State'.]

8 STC has been writing to John Taylor Coleridge for advice on his work. Now he sends him the 'first third' of *Aids to Reflection*.

10 He suggests to Allsop and to J. H. Green a series of lectures about the idea of a university, which he could give in the light of the setting up of 'a Metropolitan University' (later the University of London).

14 He writes to thank Prati for sending him a copy of G. B. Vico, in which 'I am more and more delighted'.

17 He has given up the plan of lecturing in the new London University – 'lest I should be supposed to advocate it', which,

as a Cambridge man, he feels he cannot do.

18 (Wed) STC delivers his first (and only) essay to the Royal Society of Literature, on the *Prometheus* of Aeschylus.

(late) *Aids to Reflection* published.

June

16 (Thurs) HCR, Montagu, Irving and Wrangham visit STC, who talks eloquently for several hours – though HCR cannot afterwards remember anything specific that he said and wonders if perhaps his impressive manner creates an illusion of important ideas.

30 Taylor and Hessey dissolve their partnership. Taylor retains the publishing business, but publishes no more of STC's work. STC writes to CL, claiming (wrongly) that a book of *Odes and Addresses to Great Men* which he has received must be by Lamb himself. [CL replies, explaining that the book is by Thomas Hood.]

July

8? (Fri) STC invites Daniel Stuart to 'our Highgate Thursday Conversation Evenings'.

12 He invites Blanco White (theological writer) to the Thursday evening sessions.

15 He has been preparing Henry Gillman for entry to Eton, and writes to warn Edward that the boy will be nervous, having had whooping cough.

21 STC takes Henry to Eton, where he is successfully entered into the fourth form.

He notes, on the reception of *Aids to Reflection*, that the Bishop of London likes the work, but that Hazlitt has reviewed it with his 'notorious frantic hatred of me, who was Father, and Brother to him in one'. Some time this year appears Hazlitt's *Spirit of the Age*, in which STC is presented as a betrayer of liberty and a defender of legitimacy.

September

STC writes to Edward Coleridge, continuing to build up links with 'the children of the Sons of my Father'. He is pleased this month 'to follow you in spirit along the banks of the Otter' when Edward visits Devon. STC has jaundice and cannot help Henry's preparation for Eton as he would wish. He plans to translate Bacon's *Novum Organum* for Montagu's edition of Bacon's *Works* (published by Pickering in 16 volumes, 1825–36). He doesn't do this, but he does give Montagu some help with the work, which is acknowledged in the preface.

October
5 (Wed) STC leaves for Ramsgate.
18 Henry is already in trouble at Eton. He cannot cope with the work and seems to take a pride in being punished. STC suggests to Gillman that they say that Henry's health was affected by the place and that he had to leave.
21 He spends his birthday travelling to Eton to bring back the boy.

November
STC back in Ramsgate. It has been decided that Henry should stay at Eton until Christmas.

December
20 (Tues) STC writes to his nephew John Taylor Coleridge about Derwent's 'Catterpillarage' (*sic*) in matters of faith. 'I trust in God he has been hitherto but the Larva of his final Self.' (Derwent is now 'first classical assistant at a large establishment in Buckfastleigh', according to his mother.)
21 STC writes to Derwent complaining that he never hears from him. STC is to dine with J. H. Frere, newly returned from Malta.

1826

January
CL describes STC this year as 'quite blooming'. He is still working steadily on his Opus Maximum, or justification of Trinitarian Christianity: he has finished the first treatise on logic and is engaged on the second and more important part, the Assertion of Religion. He is by now doubtful whether any publisher will accept the book in his lifetime, but he continues to work at it.
4 (Wed) Edward Lowndes, a colleague of Derwent's at Buckfastleigh School, brings STC a letter from Derwent ex-

plaining his intention to enter the Church. STC is delighted and sends him a copy of *Aids to Reflection*.

10 STC is visited by J. H. Frere who reads from his own translation of Aristophanes.

13 J. H. Frere again visits STC and takes him in his carriage to see the Marquis of Hastings at the Burlington Hotel.

19? STC writes to Frere, enclosing a copy of *Aids to Reflection* for him to give to Lord Liverpool, the Prime Minister. Frere hopes to procure for STC a sinecure of £200 a year. [However, Lord Liverpool suffers a stroke before the matter is settled and the money goes to someone else.]

(late) STC writes to Derwent, presumably because he has heard from him of his intention to marry Mary Pridham, warning him of the 'heart-withering sorrow' which can befall a young man if he finds himself incautiously committed to a young woman who does not suit him.

(late) Derwent spends three or four days at Highgate on his way back to Cambridge, where he is attending divinity lectures with a view to taking Holy Orders. STC unfortunately has influenza and cannot talk to him as he would wish.

February
(early) John Watson, another of STC's young admirers, is staying at Highgate. STC calls him my 'excellent and filial friend'. Mrs C writes to Poole that Hartley's school has closed and that he is struggling to support himself by writing.

April
(late) Daniel Stuart's wife and daughter stay at the Gillmans'. DS has had an accident, falling from a carriage. The news shakes STC considerably.

June
3 (Sat) STC visits the Aders with J. H. Frere and both are impressed by the copy Mrs Aders has made of a Van Eyck painting. She has recently recovered from an illness: STC writes 'The Two Founts' in her honour (dated 3 June 1826).

July
(early) Derwent visits again on his way to Plymouth and takes a letter from STC to his nephew Edward at Eton to deliver on the way.

19   (Wed) STC dines with CL, Frederick Reynolds and Samuel
     Bloxam. Lamb is now released from the East India Office and
     can visit STC more regularly. He is by now reconciled to
     Gillman and calls him STC's 'more than Friend'.
During this month STC is using his influence with Lady Beaumont
to procure a curacy for Derwent. He is sure that his nephew William
(now Bishop of Barbados) has 'done everything in his power to
injure me', rather than helping Derwent to a post. Sara Coleridge
was to have visited her father this month, but has been ill. Her
mother insists that she postpone the journey until September. By the
end of the month STC has learnt from Mrs Gillman of the attachment
between his daughter and her cousin. HNC has produced a book,
Six Months in the West Indies in 1825, in which he makes veiled
references to his love for a cousin; STC has read the book without
realising that the cousin is his own daughter!
27   (Thurs) STC has many visitors during these months. In a let-
     ter to nephew Edward he lists: 'Merchant, Manufacturer, Phy-
     sician, Member of Parliament & keen Politician, Chemist,
     Clergymen, *poetic* Ladies, Painters, Musical Men, Barristers
     and Political Economists'.
28   To Daniel Stuart he says that he has been 'interrupted by a run
     of Visitors from 1 at noon to 10 at night'. He asks Stuart for his
     and his wife's opinion of marriage between first cousins.

August
17   (Thurs) In Gillman's absence, STC is negotiating for C. A.
     Tulk the purchase of Winchester Hall in Highgate, put up for
     sale after the bankruptcy of the owner, Thomas Hurst.
31   His health has suffered a relapse – he is worst in his sleep, he
     says.

September
Daughter Sara pays a second visit to Highgate. She has been in poor
health and spirits and STC reluctantly agrees to an engagement with
Henry Nelson Coleridge, to end her 'miserable Heart-wasting'. The
wedding cannot take place, however, until Henry has an income: he
has just been called to the Bar.
2   (Sat) STC writes kindly to a needy author, T. J. Ouseley, re-
     gretting that he cannot help him financially or in finding a
     publisher.

8 He is still struggling to buy the Highgate house for Tulk, but finds himself like 'an unalphabeted Child' in such matters.

October
11 (Wed) STC leaves for Ramsgate for his annual holiday to improve his health – 'by the kindness of two or three friends', he says. He spends part of October, November and early December at Ramsgate, this time with Henry Gillman. Despite the efforts of STC and Edward Coleridge, it has been decided that Henry must be removed from Eton. He is to be sent to Merchant Taylors, where his brother James is head boy. [In the end he goes to Shrewsbury.] STC remarks sorrowfully to Edward: 'What has not been done or attempted for this boy!' He is worried about the health of both Mr and Mrs Gillman.
13 Gillman is thrown from his gig and injured.
28 STC writes to Edward of 'how much our family (with the single exception of myself, occasioned by my Father's sudden death) owe to your Grandmother's maternal ambition'. (One of the few recognitions of his mother's role.)
29 Derwent is ordained deacon by the Bishop of Exeter.

November
19 (Sun) STC is deeply distressed at the fate of 'my poor Firstborn'. After the failure of the Ambleside school, Hartley has sunk to a life of wandering. Mrs C has to pay his bills.

December
(early) STC has an erysipelatous inflammation of the left leg.
14 (Thurs) He returns to Highgate.

1827

January
4 (Thurs) Thomas Poole visits Highgate. Irving and Montagu are invited to meet him after dinner.

February
Daughter Sara is with her father for part of this month.

1 (Thurs) STC writes warmly to Allsop, now in deep financial trouble, inviting him to come and unburden himself.

7 Sir George Beaumont dies suddenly. He leaves Mrs C £100 and WW and RS each £100, but there is nothing for STC. STC expresses sorrow at his death, but says the omission is 'an implicit but trumpet-tongued Brand on my Honour and Character'.

9 He writes to the Council of London University in support of the candidature of his friend Hyman Hurwitz as Professor of Hebrew Language and Literature.

14 He calls on his friend, the surgeon J. B. Williams, in Town.

25 He asks Daniel Stuart for a copy of 'The Devil's Thoughts' in the original version which appeared in the *Morning Post*: it is for William Pickering, who is to publish his *Poetical Works*. [This appears in 1828.]

March

HNC continues to record STC's *Table Talk*.

10 (Sat) STC talks of Jewish history, contrasting Spinosa's ideas with Hebrew theories.

12 He talks of Roman Catholicism; energy in man and other animals; and Shakespeare's ability to characterise in a few words;

13 of the nature of understanding;

18 of parts of speech – grammar.

June

15 (Fri) STC talks of magnetism, electricity and galvanism.

24 He talks of Spenser's *Epithalamion*, the characters of Othello, Hamlet and Polonius, the Nature of Love, *Measure for Measure*, Ben Jonson. He says goodbye to his young disciple John Watson, who is going on a sea voyage to try to escape consumption. [Watson dies on 9 July aged 28.]

July

2 (Mon) STC writes to Mrs Alaric Watts that 'on Thursdays I make a point of remaining at home: as on my account & to prevent my mornings from being at the mercy of Visitors, Mr and Mrs Gillman have given a general invitation to my London and Suburban Acquaintances for Thursday Evenings, a

humble sort of Conversazione'. He wants to talk to Alaric Watts about an edition of Shakespeare with notes for the general reader and 'with the expulsion of all antiquarian Rubbish'.

8   STC talks of the Trinity.
9   He talks of the scale of animal being;
12 of the Popedom, Thomas à Becket, Ariosto and Tasso, prose and poetry.
15 (Sun) Derwent is ordained to the priesthood by the Bishop of Exeter.
20 STC talks of the non-perception of colours;
21 of the Restoration and Reformation;
23 of William III, Berkeley, Spinoza.

August
8   (Wed) Death of Canning – the 'settling blow' to STC's hopes of a pension.
29 STC talks of Jeremy Taylor; Hooker;
30 of painting, 'the intermediate somewhat between a thought and a thing'.
He tells Alaric Watts of his fears about the Pickering edition of his poems: Pickering is determined to publish everything by him, including 'much that had far better in their present state have remained unpublished'. STC feels this arrangement has been forced on him and that Gillman, whom he wants to be the beneficiary, 'will never receive a pickled herring from this Pickering'. [He is quite right – see December 1828.]

September
STC advises James Gillman Junior to adhere to a system of reading when he goes up to St John's College, Oxford.

October
Daughter Sara has spent part of the summer with her father in Highgate and is still there in early October. She then goes on to visit her cousin Edward Coleridge at Eton.
8   (Mon) STC deeply exercised over the Irish question. He feels emigration is not the answer, but rather 'bringing the waste lands & bogs into a state of Cultivation' to 'improve the quality of the remainder'. He asks Daniel Stuart humbly for the £30

he has contributed for the past three years for the annual holiday at Ramsgate.

12   He receives the £30 from Stuart.

STC again spends October and part of November at Ramsgate. He bathes for his health, dines at Sir Thomas Gray's and meets Sir William Curtis.

November

20   (Tues) STC is worried by the illnesses of Montagu and of brother George, who is 'sinking rapidly under the oppression of Dropsy in the Chest'.

24   STC writes to Leonard Horner, Warden-designate of the new University of London, due to open in October 1828, on behalf of his friend Hyman Hurwitz. He is furious that his work has been published without his knowledge in the *Bijou*, a literary annual launched by William Pickering. He had given the manuscripts to Pickering for the new *Poetical Works*; Pickering had unscrupulously handed them on to W. Frazer, the *Bijou*'s editor. The works are: 'The Wanderings of Cain: a Fragment' (later published as Canto II), and four poems: 'Work Without Hope', 'Youth and Age' (lines 1–38), 'A Daydream' and 'The Two Founts'. The *Bijou* also extracted and published without STC's knowledge a sonnet dedicated to him by Blanco White.

Thursday evening conversation sessions now take place regularly at Highgate. John Sterling comes for the first time probably during this year and writes of the 'glittering eye' of the 'Ancient Mariner'. Thomas Carlyle also leaves a famous description, calling STC a man of 'great and useless genius'. Other visitors are Basil Montagu, Edward Irving, J. H. Green, Henry Taylor, Charles Aders, William Collins the painter, Thomas Chalmers and Henry Nelson Coleridge. Lamb comes occasionally, but prefers the peace of Sunday evening visits.

December

6   (Thurs) Derwent, who now has a curacy at Helston, marries Mary Pridham. (STC has written her a poem, 'Dear, though unseen'.)

1828

January

This year Hyman Hurwitz is appointed Professor of Hebrew at London University.

12 (Sat) George Coleridge dies. STC, when he hears, writes affectionately to George's son, George May Coleridge, 'as one who loved in him Father and Brother in one'. He declares that 'Never have man's feelings and character been more cruelly misrepresented than mine . . . the belief of my brother's alienation and the grief that I was a stranger in the house of my second father has been the secret wound that to this hour never closed or healed up.'

25 STC writes about his physical symptoms to J. H. Green. His leg will not heal and he suspects scirrhus in the kidney.

February

STC now has erysipelas in both legs and 'considerable oedema' in his right leg, producing 'intolerable Itching' and disturbance of sleep.

19 (Tues) STC writes in delight to 'My very dear children', Derwent and Mary, that he has finally arranged for the long-overdue payment to Derwent of the arrears of the Lady North Exhibition awarded by the Mercers' Company and held by him since 1822. [The matter had been delayed because STC had mistaken some letters from the Mercers' Company for those of the Royal Society of Literature and never opened them!] He dines at J. H. Green's and reads and laughs at Leigh Hunt's article on him in the newly published *Lord Byron and Some of His Contemporaries*.

March

17 (Mon) STC talks at length to Lady Beaumont at her London home. She urges him to resume writing poetry (see May 1828).

20 STC writes to the Scottish poet Thomas Pringle that he has for four or five months been enraptured by the latter's 'Afar in the Desart': 'For some days I did little else but read and recite your poem.' He invites Pringle to the Thursday evening gatherings – from 6 to 10 or 11'.

April
Perhaps moved by George's death, STC's brother James visits him in Highgate. [Three of James's sons, Henry Nelson, John Taylor and Edward, are all now part of the STC circle.] STC writes to the *Quarterly Review* suggesting that he contribute a review of Napier's *History of the Peninsula War*, volume 1. He retells the anecdote that he had written what he thought were witty reviews as a young man, but was so taken aback by DW's reaction to them that he never afterwards wrote another review.

22 (Tues) STC at Sotheby's where he meets Sir Walter Scott and James Fenimore Cooper.

(end) Cooper and Sotheby visit him at Highgate.

May
STC is reading the *Medical Gazette* and discussing medical matters with J. H. Green. He also discusses whether Green should accept the Chair of Surgery at the newly-established King's College, London. STC suspects, rightly, that this College is the response of the 'defenders of the established order' – especially the Duke of Wellington – to the Whigs' challenge in setting up University College.

27 (Tues) He has finished the synopsis to his Opus Maximum.

June
STC responds to George Dyer's request for a meeting by inviting him and his family to one of the Thursday evenings – referring to him as 'my dear long-known and long-loved Friend!' The WWs are in London and have met STC.

18 (Wed) STC and WW breakfast with Crabb Robinson at Charles Aders: they have suddenly agreed to a tour of the Rhineland with WW's daughter Dora (STC's god-daughter). HCR notes that STC is 'very eloquent as usual in his dreamy monologues'. STC criticises RS (now Poet Laureate) for allowing himself to be flattered by Peel. Aders helps arrange passports and letters of credit.

22 STC, WW and Dora depart for Ostend.

25 They reach Brussels, where they meet the novelist T. C. Grattan.

July
They travel via the field of Waterloo to Namur, thence by barge to Liège, then by Spa, Aix-le-Chapelle and Cologne to Godesberg (now Bad Godesberg).

3 (Tues) They stay with Aders' wife, who is at the family château in Godesberg. Mrs Aders, a singer, is 'delighted' with WW but regards 'our old affectionate friend Coleridge' as 'her' poet. The poet A. W. von Schlegel visits them and praises STC's translation of Schiller's *Wallenstein*. He takes them to his house in Bonn, where he is Professor of Literature.

11 They leave Godesberg to journey up the Rhine to Bingen, then return to Godesberg for several days.

They then go on to Nijmegen by steamboat, to Arnheim and Utrecht by coach, to Amsterdam, Haarlem, Leiden, The Hague, Delft and Rotterdam by barge; to Antwerp by steamer; thence to Ghent and by barge to Ostend.

August
6 (Wed) The three travellers return to WW's lodgings with Quillinan at 12 Bryanston Street.

During this month *The Poetical Works of STC* in three volumes are published by Pickering. They contain the 'Ancient Mariner', 'Christabel', 'Kubla Khan', 'The Pains of Sleep', *Sybilline Leaves, Remorse, Zapolya, Wallenstein* and selected juvenilia. Only 300 copies are printed. HNC visits the north. STC sends 'my best Love to Mr and Mrs WW and Miss W and Miss Sara Hutchinson' and 'to those at Keswick what can I say other than that their happiness & comforts are an indispensable condition & part of [his own] well-being and peace of mind'. He prepares a contribution to *The Keepsake*, edited by Frederic M. Reynolds. Rudolph Ackermann, publisher of *The Forget Me Not*, an illustrated annual, solicits a contribution from STC, who refuses because of his contract with Reynolds of *The Amulet* not to give or sell any contributions to both annuals.

18 (Mon) STC is the star of a bachelor dinner-party at the lodgings of F. M. Reynolds. Lockhart, Theodore Hook and William Jerdan are also there. Hook improvises a comic song with a reference to STC in every line. Much claret is drunk, and Hook and STC each break a pane of glass by throwing their wine glasses at the window.

At a more sober dinner-party at Sotheby's, STC meets Walter Scott and launches into a disquisition on the multiple authorship of the *Iliad*. 'Zounds, I was never more bethumped for words!' records Scott.

September
*c.*16–17 STC pays his long-delayed visit to CL at Enfield. He goes
           for long walks 'beyond Cheshunt' and brings on the erysipelas
           in his leg again.

October
The 300 copies of the *Poetical Works* are 'sold off' with, as STC
predicted, no profits left for himself or Gillman.
14   (Tues) He writes again to Stuart for money for his Ramsgate
     holiday. Stuart sends £20.
17   His first grandchild, Derwent Moultrie Coleridge, is born.
STC again spends the end of October and all of November at Ramsgate
(9 Waterloo Plains).

December
Alaric Watts tries to persuade STC to write exclusively for his *Literary Souvenir* for 1830. STC feels he is under contract to Reynolds and
The Keepsake and, encouraged by Reynolds, declines the offer. Thus
ends his association with Watts.
3   (Wed) Mrs Morgan visits him, begging him to find £20 for her
    and her sister.
4   STC writes to S. C. Hall on behalf of John Morgan's widow
    and sister-in-law, who are struggling against poverty. He is
    busy 'trotting about' among friends to make up £20 for them.

1829

January
19   (Mon) STC writes to Thomas Hurst asking him to check the
     terms he has drawn up with John Taylor the publisher for a
     second edition of *Aids to Reflection*, two volumes of a *System of
     the Faith and Philosophy of STC* and a volume on the *Use of
     Words*.
He receives £30 from Pickering as an advance on the new edition of
the *Poetical Works*; he sends £20 of this to Mrs Morgan (see December
1828). He refuses to sign a petition against Catholic emancipation.

February
12   (Thurs) At the Thursday evening meeting are Henry Taylor,

John Romilly, John Stuart Mill (who later this year reviews the *Poetical Works* and who makes other visits to Highgate), W. Hutt ('a great traveller'), Edward Irving 'with two Scotch Divines', Adam Steinmetz, Dr Watson and an American artist who wishes to be introduced to STC.

20   STC is forced by ill health to give up work on the second volume of *Aids to Reflection*. There are ominous signs of erysipelas on his forehead. 'This was the death-signal of my friend Sir George Beaumont', he says. He therefore declines the offer to produce work for F. A. Cox of the University of London, in case 'I should be in my winding sheet'.

March
23   (Mon) HNC has been dangerously ill. STC's illness continues, but he has been able to work at *On the Constitution of the Church and the State* – there are only a few pages left to complete.

April
(late)   Mrs C and daughter Sara arrive at Rydal Mount and stay with the WWs for about a month. Poole has visited Highgate and sends Mrs C a favourable account of STC's health.

May
(early)   STC is at last convalescent and writes to support Thomas Allsop in a trading scheme to do with a 'New Settlement' – though he expresses severe doubts about its practicality. He puts Allsop in touch with Henry Taylor at the Colonial Office.

July
STC's health has been so bad that he has for the moment given up his Thursday evening meetings. He advises John Anster, one of his disciples, not to marry eighteen-year-old Susan Steel. (Anster is 36 and not yet financially secure.) He mentions that a 'young Oxonian' is also courting her. This is James Gillman Junior. He advises James at the same time to get to know Susan very well before committing himself to such an irrevocable step as marriage, quoting Genesis 2.24: 'They shall be one Flesh.'

13   (Mon) He encloses in a letter to RS 'Lines on a Lady's Album', which are later published in *The Keepsake*, 1830.
14   Lady Beaumont dies. She leaves STC £50, which he sends to Mrs C for Hartley.

29   WW informs Montagu that Hartley has been staying with
     Professor Wilson, where he behaved well apart from a disap-
     pearance of a few days 'arising from a cause which is one [we]
     can guess at'.
(late) STC sends Reynolds the conclusion to his ballad *Alice du Clos*,
which Reynolds and Heath want to publish in the 1830 *Keepsake*.
They don't pay him anything, as his contribution to the 1829 edition
was four pages short.

August
STC is suffering severely from sciatica and has to cancel a proposed
visit to Helsdon to see his first grandchild, Derwent Moultrie
Coleridge. He writes to Thomas H. Dunn, chemist and druggist of
Highgate, for morphine.
6   (Thurs) He writes acrimoniously to Reynolds, who has criti-
    cised Gillman for being 'officious' over his friend's affairs: he
    protests about the lack of remuneration for his 1830 *Keepsake*
    contribution. He asks for the return of *Alice du Clos* as he
    wishes to substitute two other poems.

September
STC proposes transferring the second edition of *Aids to Reflection*
from John Taylor to Hurst, Chance and Co.
1   (Tues) HNC arrives at Keswick.
3   Sara Coleridge and Henry Nelson Coleridge are at last mar-
    ried, at Crosthwaite outside Keswick. John Wordsworth, Sara's
    childhood playmate, now in the Church, conducts the service
    and Dora Wordsworth is bridesmaid.
Mrs C now leaves Greta Hall (see May 1830).
17   STC writes his will.

October
STC writes to the publishers Hurst and Chance about the possibility
of including another chapter in *On the Constitution of the Church
and the State* – 'What is to be done now?' [It is later added as an
appendix.]
20   (Tues) He writes to *Blackwood's Magazine* with a list of ar-
     ticles he could send them; he expresses admiration for the
     magazine.

December
STC complains of rheumatic fever, coming in fits, and preceded by 'an indescribable depression of Spirits which my Reason finds it difficult to overrule'. Hurst, Chance and Co. publish *On the Constitution of the Church and the State.*
Some time this year a new and much-corrected edition of the *Poetical Works* appears.

1830

STC's health continues to deteriorate and from now until the end of his life he spends most of his time in his attic bedroom, suffering from sciatica, rheumatism and severe digestive problems, all presumably made worse by opium addiction.

February
The WWs report that Hartley is living like a vagabond and sleeping in barns.
13   (Sun) STC receives a poor poet, Charles Whitehead, who has sent him his manuscript. He does this out of kindness, as he suspects Whitehead is 'a poor man as well as a very poor Poet'.

March
DW tells Mrs C, who is staying in Cornwall with Derwent's family, that Hartley's debts have been paid and he has been found accommodation with the Flemings at Town End, Grasmere.

April
WW reports that Hartley has been found several times lying intoxicated in the road. STC writes to H. W. Montagu complaining at his publishing 'The Devil's Thoughts' (written by STC and RS in 1799) as 'The Devil's Walk: a poem by Professor Porson'. HNC continues to make notes of STC's conversations for *Table Talk.*
13   (Tues) STC talks of the Old Testament Prophets, the Messiah and the Trinity;
14   of the conversion of the Jews;
17   of Mosaic miracles and Pantheism;
18   of poetic promise;

19   of his attitude to death ('I never had any horror of Death, simply as death');

30   of Nominalists and Realists; of British Schoolmen; of Spinosa.

May

The second edition of *On the Constitution of the Church and of the State* is published. Sara and HNC settle in a small house in Hampstead. After 30 years in Keswick, Mrs C joins them there. STC writes to Hurst, Chance and Co. to advise them about their plans for a 'New Comic Annual' in 1831. He dislikes the title and suggests various others, including 'Sir John Falstaff's Annual' [which they eventually use as a subtitle]. HNC, now living nearby, records STC's *Table Talk* virtually every night this month.

1   (Sat) STC talks of the Fall of Man; of madness; of Brown and Darwin; of nitrous oxide;

2   of plants, insects, man;

3   he desires 'an inscription on my tomb, that I was an enthusiastic lover of Christ';

4   of Holland and the Dutch;

7   of Horne Tooke;

8   of Horne Tooke; the Jacobins. At 10 pm STC writes a letter of heartfelt thanks to Mrs Gillman, giving her his blessing. He seems to have a premonition of his own death and is 'weighed down by a heavy presentment respecting my own sojourn here'. At about this time he has a seizure and collapses in his room. He is revived, and says on opening his eyes, 'What a mystery we are!' He is now convinced that he will die in his sleep, 'as my dear father did, whose very facsimile I am, both in body and mind'. [John Coleridge died at 62 – as STC was to do.]

9   STC talks of Persian and Arabic poetry.

10   He takes a strong interest in the fate of the Free Grammar School in Highgate and the building of a new chapel for its use.

11   He talks of Sir Thomas Munro, Sir Stafford Raffles and Canning;

12   of Shakespeare, Milton and Homer;

14   of Reason and Understanding; of words and the names of things;

15   of the Trinity. He writes to *Blackwood's* that he has destroyed

the £10 order they have sent him, as he has not written the articles he promised.

16 He talks of Abraham, Isaac and Jacob;
17 of the origins of acts; of love;
18 of grammar schools; of Democracy;
20 of the Eucharist; of the divinity of Christ;
21 of talent and genius; of motives and impulses;
23 of hysteria; of hydro-carbonic gas; of specific medicines;
25 of the Epistles to the Ephesians and the Colossians;
27 of flogging;
28 of the Americans;
29 of the Book of Job;
30 of translations of the Psalms;
31 of the 'Ancient Mariner'; of *Undine*; of the painter John Martin; of the *Pilgrim's Progress*.
31 The Professor of Theology at the University of Edinburgh, Dr Thomas Chalmers, visits STC, bringing his wife and daughter. He writes to Green for help in finding a job for the brother of Harriet Macklin, the Gillmans' servant, who is devoted to him.

June

STC is in the habit of borrowing *The Times* from Thomas Hurst, who lives nearby.

1 (Thurs) STC talks of prayer; of church-singing; of Hooker; and of dreams.
2 He writes to Poole that he has been on 'the brink of the grave' and sends him a copy of the second edition of *On the Constitution of the Church and of the State* [though he doesn't draw his attention to his description of Poole in the note to page 115 of the book].
4 He talks of Jeremy Taylor and of the English Reformation;
6 of Catholicity, gnosis, Tertullian and St John;
7 of the principles behind setting up a review; of party-spirit;
10 of RS's Life of Bunyan; of Archbishop Laud; of Puritans and Cavaliers; of Presbyterians, Independents and bishops;
14 of the study of the Bible;
15 of Rabelais and Swift; of Bentley and Burnet;
25 of Giotto and of the place of painting in a society;
26 of Seneca.

July
- 2 (Fri) STC adds a codicil to his will that any money left for Hartley be kept in trust for him. He talks of Plato and Aristotle ('every man is born an Aristotelian, or a Platonist');
- 4 of the Duke of Wellington; of moneyed interest; of Canning;
- 6 of Bourrienne ('the French Pepys');
- 8 of the Jews;
- 24 of the Papacy and the Reformation;
- 26 of John Thelwall; of Swift and Stella;
- 28 of iniquitous legislation;
- 29 of Spurzheim (German craniologist).

August
- 20 (Fri) STC talks of the French Revolution; of the English and American characters.

September
- 8 (Wed) STC talks of the English Reformation.
- 18 Death of William Hazlitt. STC adapts a bitter epigram about him, but hopes the Almighty will receive him.
- 19 He talks of democracy; of the idea of the State and of the Church.
- 20 of Government; and of the French *gendarmerie*;
- 21 of the philosophy of young men at the present day;
- 22 of Thucydides; of Tacitus; of poetry and modern metre;
- 23 of logic;
- 24 of Varro; of Socrates; of Greek philosophy; of Plotinus and Tertullian;
- 26 of Scottish and English laws;
- 27 of love and friendship contrasted; of marriage; of the characteristics of women;
- 28 of mental anarchy.

October
- 5 (Tues) STC talks of love of music; of the English liturgy; of the Belgian Revolution.
- 7 or 8 Daughter Sara's first child, Herbert, is born (possibly named after RS's son who died at the age of 10 in 1816).
- 8 STC talks of Galileo, Newton, Kepler and Bacon;
- 20 of the Reformation.

November

29 (Mon) STC writes to H. F. Cary asking for help in ascertaining 'the causes of the Obscurity felt generally in my prose writings'.

30 He talks of the House of Commons.

December

STC writes to John Reade that he wishes that he had met Shelley in Keswick in 1811–12. RS did instead. Shelley 'would have felt that I understood him. His Atheism would not have scared me.'

1 (Wed) He writes to his son-in-law HNC, worried that the latter has caught cold by taking the outside place on the coach up to visit him. [HNC's health is indeed precarious: he dies within a few years of his father-in-law.]

22 He writes to Mrs W. L. Rogers that he will exert his influence in procuring a professorship for her brother, John Frederic Daniell, in King's College, London, which will be opening in 1831. [Daniell is eventually appointed Professor of Chemistry.]

24 WW is in London and visits STC in Highgate. This is probably one of several meetings during his stay. The two never meet again.

1831

January

Final meetings with WW during the latter's stay in London. In the intense controversy over the Reform Bill this year, STC is bitterly opposed to the Bill, though he is not against the idea of reform itself. Derwent visits Highgate. He is thinking of taking a large private school in Harrow, but decides against it. STC has read the *Quarterly Review* article (October 1830) on the first volume of Charles Lyell's *Principles of Geology* and is sceptical of it. (His nephew John Taylor Coleridge is now editor of the *Quarterly Review*.)

March

20 (Sun) STC talks of government; and of Earl Grey's role in reform.

May

Almost a year after the death of George IV and the accession of
William IV, the Royal Associates of the Society of Literature are told
that their annual grants of 100 guineas are to be discontinued. STC
appeals through Sotheby to Lord Brougham, the Chancellor, and
Rogers and Lamb separately appeal to Earl Grey, the First Lord of
the Treasury. Grey offers STC £200 in two annual grants.

  27   (Fri) STC asks HNC's advice about accepting Grey's offer. He
       feels it is insulting: 'I have a respite of a full year before my
       deposition in the Workhouse.'

June

  1?   STC writes to Sotheby for advice on the £200 offer. He speaks
       of his 'honourable Poverty' which is the effect of 'an entire and
       faithful dedication of myself to Ends and Objects' for which he
       believed himself to especially fitted, and a consequent giving-
       up of more lucrative employment.

  3   (Fri) Sotheby receives STC's letter and immediately calls on
       him, offering him a gift of £50 and trying to persuade him to
       accept the £200. However, encouraged by Gillman, STC refuses
       Grey's offer. Gillman sends a letter to *The Times* explaining
       STC's decision. From now on, J. H. Frere makes an annual gift
       to STC to compensate for the loss.

  25   STC talks of the great ends of government and of popular
       representation: he agrees there is need for reform but is afraid
       of 'a degrading delegation of the populace'.

  26   He talks of Colonel Napier; of Bonaparte; and of RS.

July

  7   (Thurs) STC talks of the patronage of the fine arts – appallingly
       absent in England, he says.

  24   He talks of painting. He has visited an exhibition of Old Mas-
       ters at the British Gallery in Pall Mall with HNC, who records
       his comments on Claude, Teniers and Rubens.

  25   He talks of Chillingworth's book on protestantism; of the su-
       perstition of the Maltese, Sicilians and Italians;

  30   of Asgill's pamphlet on eternal life; of prejudice against the
       French.

August

  1   (Mon) STC talks of the beast and the devil in man;

6   of the good and the true (women often love the good for its
     own sake, but seldom the truth. It is essential to see them as
     identical);
8   of England and Holland; of iron, galvanism and heat;
14   of national and colonial character.
21   He accepts the invitation to be god-father to the baby daughter
     of Charles Stutfield.

September
13   (Tues) STC writes to J. H. Green against the Reform Bill (about
     to have its Third Reading in Parliament). He objects to the
     campaign in the press in its support, calling it 'hellish Licence',
     and speaking of 'the system of intimidation carried on by the
     Journalists and Pamphleteers'.
22   Henry Taylor brings J. S. Mill and James Stephen to visit STC.

November
19   (Sat) STC writes discouragingly to the artist David Scott who
     wishes to illustrate the 'Ancient Mariner'. He says he has no
     knowledge of or influence with publishers: 'I question whether
     there ever existed a man of letters so utterly friendless.'
During this year STC prepares a second edition of *Aids to Reflection*,
helped by HNC, and published by Hurst, Chance and Co.

1832

STC suffers increasing ill health, but is cheered by his continued
mental clarity and by the fact that by the spring, he has 'no craving
for the Poison' (that is, opium). [But see next entry.]

January
6   (Fri) STC sends a bottle to T. H. Dunn, the chemist, to be filled
     with 'Tinct. Op.' (opium).
10   He writes with wise advice to James Gillman junior and Susan
     Steel, approving of their betrothal but recommending delay
     until the 'rightful conditions' for the marriage pertain.
11   Although he is still sick and depressed, he writes a comic ode
     to his 'little black Shaving Pot', which the maid, Harriet, has
     replaced.

25   He investigates the possibility of receiving money from the bankrupt estate of the publishers, Rest Fenner. [He later receives £102.]

February
STC is very interested in the cholera epidemic and writes learnedly to Green about it.
11   (Sat) He thinks up an anti-government cartoon depicting the ruin, as he sees it, brought about by the Reform Bill.

March
STC tells Green that he now has an aversion to opium.
18   (Sun) Professor William Hamilton, of Trinity College, Dublin, calls to see STC but he is too ill to receive visitors.
20   Hamilton calls again and is received.
23   Hamilton makes a second visit.

April
An American edition of *Aids to Reflection* is now out and some American admirers come to Highgate, including H. B. McLellan of Harvard, who notices STC's 'careless dress, venerable locks of white hair and trembling frame'.
4   (Wed) STC tries to find the first volume of Kant's *Miscellaneous Essays*, but cannot, 'in the wilderness of my books'.
12   HCR and Mrs Aders drive to see STC, who is in bed but looks 'beautifully . . . his eye remarkably brilliant'. He declaims against the Reform Bill, saying that the government should not yield simply for fear of the mob.
22   He apologises to H. F. Cary for his 'very rude and uncourteous vehemence of contradiction' when Cary supported the Reform Bill. He says that God has worked a miracle of grace on him by releasing him from '33 years' fearful Slavery' to opium.
He plans to write on John Asgill, 'a prime Darling of mine – the most honest of the Whigs' (in the early 1700s), whose *Tracts* he adores. [Nothing comes of this.]

May
STC has been reading and enjoying 'my old friend De Quincey's *Klosterheim*'. Much better, he says, than anything Scott has produced. He praises *Blackwood's Magazine* as 'the only remaining link between the Periodical press and the enduring literature of Great Britain'.

17 (Thurs) He puts off a visit from Green, as he has had a relapse:
    'I am in a state . . . in which you could not help being shocked,
    without the least chance of doing me any good.'

June
STC refers to his 'old bad habits' of not opening letters – because of
'a sort of cowardly awe and superstitious reverence for the Seals'.

July
2 (Mon) Daughter Sara's second child, Edith, is born. From this
   time Sara's health breaks down.
HNC begins to prepare a cheaper, third edition of the *Poetical Works*.
[This comes out in 1834.]

August
STC is now taking 'Air Baths' at Great Marlborough Street under
Dr Jonathan Green.
9 (Thurs) STC attends the christening of his new grandchild,
   Edith, with James Gillman junior officiating. He tells Green
   how much he wants to stand beside Mrs C during the service:
   'In fact, bating living in the same house with her, there are few
   women that I have a greater respect and ratherish liking for,
   than Mrs C.' Mrs C herself writes proudly to Poole after the
   meeting that STC 'has entirely left off the use of opium'.
13 STC hears of the death of his young disciple, Adam Steinmetz,
   who leaves him a legacy of £300. STC writes to Steinmetz's
   father to satisfy himself that the young man was in sound
   mind when he made the will, before he will accept the money.
   He also writes affectingly to Steinmetz's close friend,
   J. P. Kennard, of 'a loss too awful for common grief', and
   invites Kennard to visit him at any time. [JPK later names
   his second son Adam Steinmetz and STC is god-father – see
   September 1833 and 13 July 1834].

September
12 (Wed) STC makes a rare trip from Highgate to sit for the artist
   Moses Haughton in Great Marlborough Street.
29 HCR, Walter Savage Landor and Julius Hare visit STC and
   find him 'horribly bent' and looking '70 years of age'. Much of
   his conversation, reports HCR, is repetition of earlier ideas.

December
STC writes to T. H. Dunn, the chemist, for opium [belying his assertions during the year.]

1833

STC's health improves this year. He receives Harriet Martineau (they argue over political economy) and Ralph Waldo Emerson, whose visit is not a success as STC criticises Unitarianism, which Emerson holds dear.

January
STC speaks of Mrs Hathaway's legacy, which is small and which he intends to halve with Mrs C.

February
5   (Tues) WW hears from HCR that STC is unwell.

April
STC describes his day to Green in his 'average of my endurable state'. He admits he takes 'two very small teaspoonsful of Laudanum only once in 24 Hours – not a third of what I used to take twice a day'.

June
STC writes to Thomas Pringle, secretary of the Anti-slavery Society, declaring himself to be 'an ardent & almost life-long Denouncer of Slavery'.
(late)   He goes with Gillman and Green to a meeting of the British Association in Cambridge, where he meets Derwent, a new disciple, William Rowan Hamilton, and his old school-fellow, Charles le Grice.

July
Hartley's first volume of poems is published, dedicated to his father. STC is back in Ramsgate, at 4 Belle Vue Place, with the Gillmans and Henry. He frequently meets John Gibson Lockhart and his wife Sophie (daughter of Sir Walter Scott). He feels ten years younger in spirit.
26   (Fri) STC, who describes himself as 'a favourite among the Descendants of Abraham', is invited to the Synagogue in

Ramsgate. He is introduced to Moses Montefiore, its founder, whose father, says STC, is 'without exception the most beautiful old man I ever saw'. Harriet Martineau visits STC.

August

5 (Mon) Ralph Waldo Emerson visits STC. STC, improved in health by 'warm salt Shower baths', wishes HNC and Sara could afford them. 'I am always thinking and dreaming about Sara.'

6 (Tues) He sends an early poem, 'My Baptismal Birthday', and a fragment, 'On stern Blencathra's perilous Height', to Thomas Pringle, editor of *Friendship's Offering*. [They are published in the 1834 edition.] Later in the month he also sends 'Love's Apparition'.

18 He asks Charles Aders if he knows of any copying machine to be had cheaply.

September

(early) STC travels to Hackney to stand godfather to the infant son of J. P. Kennard, named Adam Steinmetz after STC's young friend and disciple.

October

(late) STC writes his own epitaph, 'Stop, Christian passer-by!' He sends copies to J. H. Green, Mrs Charles Aders, John Sterling and J. G. Lockhart.

29 (Tues) He writes to Gioacchino de' Prati in support of another Italian political agitator, Filippo Buonarotti. He is in favour of their reformist cause.

November

STC plans to buy a complete Quarto Bible and Apocrypha, intending to read one or more chapters every night during 1834. He writes to his daughter Sara, who has been seriously ill and is pregnant again.

1834

January

1 (Wed) STC sends a New Year gift to Dinah Knowe, the Gillmans' faithful maid.

4   STC asks HNC to write to Pickering in praise of the revived
    Gentleman's Magazine (to which, he says, in its old form, his
    father, John Coleridge, had written).
(early)   Daughter Sara gives birth to twins, Berkeley and Florence,
both of whom die on 16 January.

March
Poetical Works in three volumes published March–July.
17 (Mon) STC displays a red streak of erysipelas on his cheek –
    'the very thing that carried off my Acquaintance-friend Sir
    George Beaumont'; he writes at once to ask J. H. Green to visit
    him: 'I should like at once to see you before I went, if go I am
    – & leave with you, the sole Depositarium of my Mind and
    Aspirations, what God may suggest to me.'

May
27 (Tues) STC writes a testimonial for the Reverend James
    Gillman, elder son of his benefactor, for the living of Leiston
    (Gillman is unsuccessful).
Thomas Poole visits during this month and spends 'some hours'
with STC, finding his mind 'as strong as ever, seeming impatient to
take leave of its encumbrance'. A few days later Sara H visits STC.

June
STC writes to Eliza Nixon (a young neighbour?), thanking her for
her gift of flowers.

July
13 (Sun) STC writes his last letter – to his infant godchild, Adam
    Steinmetz Kennard, affirming the truths of Christianity and
    referring to himself as 'on the brink of the grave' but with 'the
    inward peace that passeth all understanding'.
19 STC falls very ill this evening.
20 HNC is sent for next morning and carries STC's blessings back
    to his wife and daughter. They are not summoned nor his sons
    sent for, as Gillman and Green feel family interviews would
    be too much for STC, who has expressed a desire to be left
    alone to meditate on his Redeemer. He does not even wish to
    see Dr Green. Mr Taylor, Dr Gillman's assistant, attends STC
    in order to spare Gillman.

24 STC sees Mrs Gillman for the last time (she has to be carried in to see him as she has a broken leg). At 7.30 p.m. he writes a note asking that a legacy be collected for his faithful servant, Harriet Macklin. Half an hour later, Gillman sees him raise his head as if in prayer and then fall into a sleep which soon turns into a coma. Green (and Gillman?) stay with him through the night.

25 STC dies at 6.30 a.m. An autopsy is held as STC had requested. It is discovered that his heart is greatly enlarged; this has probably been the cause of his long bodily sufferings.

27 The news of STC's death reaches the WWs via HNC.

28 MW takes the news to Hartley, who then calls at Rydal Mount, seeming to grieve that he has spent so little time with his father. (They have not seen each other for ten years.)

August
2 (Sat) STC is buried at Highgate Cemetery. The family are represented by HNC and Edward Coleridge, and the disciples by Green, Charles Stutfield and John Sterling, who travels from Cambridge. Gillman is too ill to come and Mrs Gillman cannot. CL is inconsolable and cannot bring himself to attend. STC's will, composed in 1829, leaves his property, consisting almost entirely of the insurance policy, now worth £2560, as well as the publishing rights in his manuscripts and letters, to Green in trust for his wife and children. There are notes of esteem for WW, RS and Frere; gifts to Sara, Derwent's wife Mary and the Gillmans; mourning rings for CL, Montagu, Poole, Josiah Wade and his son Lancelot, and Sara H. In a codicil of 1830, in his own hand, he instructs that any share coming to Hartley be kept in trust for him.

November
(early) Mrs C pays a short visit to the Gillmans. She reports to Poole that 'they find it difficult to reconcile themselves to their loss'. They have erected a tablet to STC in Highgate churchyard.

December
27 (Sat) Charles Lamb dies. [WW later links the two in his 'Extempore Effusion on the death of James Hogg', November 1835.]

1835

June

24 (Thurs) Sara H dies at Rydal Mount, 'leaving upon her face as heavenly an expression in the peace and silence of death as ever human Creature had', writes WW to HCR next day.

Postscript

Shortly after STC's death, Southey took it upon himself to describe the feelings at Greta Hall: 'All who were of his blood were in the highest degree proud of his reputation, but this was their only feeling concerning him'. Wordsworth, in contrast, was deeply moved. In November 1835 he wrote in his 'Extempore Effusion upon the Death of James Hogg':

> Nor has the rolling year twice measured,
> From sign to sign, its steadfast course,
> Since every mortal power of Coleridge
> Was frozen at its marvellous source;
>
> The rapt One, of the godlike forehead,
> The heaven-eyed creature sleeps in earth:
> And Lamb, the frolic and the gentle,
> Has vanished from his lonely hearth.

Mrs Coleridge continued to live with her daughter until her death in 1845. Sara and Henry Nelson Coleridge moved in 1837 from their cottage in Hampstead to a more comfortable house, Chester Place in Regent's Park. There the loyal son-in-law continued to work as STC's literary executor. He produced *Table Talk* in 1835, four volumes of *Literary Remains*, two in 1836 and two more in 1838, and *Confessions of an Inquiring Spirit* in 1840. However, in 1841 his own precarious health broke down and he died of spinal paralysis in January 1843. His wife devoted the brief remainder of what by all accounts was a saintly life to her two children, Herbert and Edith, and to editorial work offered at once to a husband's and a father's memory. In 1844 she produced a one-volume edition of the *Poems*; in 1847 came a second edition of *Biographia Literaria* with her own and her husband's notes; and in 1850 she published three volumes of *Essays on his Own Times*. Her own health had always been fragile and after a long illness she died on 3 May 1852. Immediately after her death, Edward Moxon published the 'new edition' of the *Poems* which she had been preparing during her last months.

Hartley Coleridge, always a waif and a wanderer, died at Grasmere in 1849, attended by Derwent. Wordsworth chose the spot for his grave, at the same time indicating where he himself was to be placed (as it turned out, just over a year later).

Derwent Coleridge, during a long and successful career, satisfied all the claims of filial and brotherly piety. He produced a Life of his brother in 1849 and in 1851 published Hartley's *Essays and Marginalia*. He also took up the baton passed on by his brother-in-law and sister, issuing his father's *Dramatic Works* in 1852 and producing two new editions of the *Poems* in 1863 and 1870. He wrote copiously on religious matters and, as Principal of St Mark's College, Chelsea, helped 'to shape elementary education in England' (*Dictionary of National Biography*). He died in 1883 at the age of 82.

Select Who's Who

These brief notes are intended to amplify references in the Chronology, particularly to individuals not in the public domain. The well-known figures of Wordsworth, Lamb, Southey, Byron, De Quincey and Hazlitt are excluded, as are Mary Lamb and Dorothy Wordsworth, since information about them is readily available elsewhere.

Adams, Dr Joseph (1756–1818), physician and editor of the *Medical and Physical Journal*, published a book on cancer in 1795. In 1805 he became physician to the Smallpox Hospital in London. He recommended STC to the care of James Gillman in 1816.

Aders, Mr and Mrs Charles Mr Aders was a wealthy German merchant who lived in Euston Square and owned valuable paintings. STC met him during the Highgate years. Mrs Aders, née Eliza Smith, was a daughter of John Raphael Smith, painter and engraver. STC addressed his poem 'The Two Founts' to her. The Aders' home housed a fine collection of Italian, early Flemish and German paintings. Samuel Palmer visited in the 1820s, as did Charles Lamb, who wrote a poem describing it as a chapel.

Allen Robert (1772–1805), known as 'Bob Allen', was an army surgeon and journalist. He was at Christ's Hospital with STC, and went on as a sizar to University College, Oxford, where STC visited him in 1794; Allen introduced him to Southey of Balliol. He became interested in Pantisocracy, but defected by the end of the year. STC wrote in his defence to Southey, 'He did never promise to form one of our party' (*Letters*, I. 146). He later married a widow with daughters as old as himself. STC sent him money when he was in great financial distress in 1796, commenting that Allen had sent him food and wept over him during his time in the army (*Letters*, I. 265). Under the influence of Godwin he became an atheist. He died of apoplexy while STC was in Malta; told of his death, STC sank into melancholy. Lamb refers to his 'happy laugh and handsome face'. There is a story about his good looks in Leigh Hunt's *Autobiography* (1850, ch. 3).

Allsop, Thomas (1795–1880), began as a silk-merchant and eventually became a rich stockbroker. He met STC in 1818 at Highgate, where, in his own words, he was STC's 'favourite disciple'. He fell into temporary financial difficulties in 1827 and saw little of STC thereafter. In 1836 he published *Letters, Conversations and Recollections of Coleridge*, which contains good stories of Lamb but is unreliable about STC.

Allston, Washington (1779–1843) was an American historical painter and poet. STC met him in Rome on his way back from Malta in 1805. Later he came to London and painted STC's portrait, now in the National Portrait Gallery. He was a friend of WW and Southey too. His best-known paintings are 'Jacob's Dream' and 'Uriel in the Sun'.

Ball, Sir Alexander (1757–1809) was a distinguished naval figure who forced the capitulation of the French at Malta in 1800 after a two-year blockade. He became the first Governor of Malta and died there. STC was delighted to have the benefit of his society and to work for him.

Banks, Sir Joseph (1743–1820), a great Lincolnshire figure: explorer, naturalist, President of the Royal Society. STC applied to him in 1803 for Indian hemp ('bang') to help alleviate the sufferings of Thomas Wedgwood.

Barbauld, Anna Letitia (1743–1825) was a poet, author of books for children and miscellaneous writer who supported radical causes. STC met her in Bristol in 1797 and at first admired her work and her ability to keep 'within the bounds of practical Reason', which he felt he could not do (*Letters*, I. 578). However, in a lecture in January 1812 he is reported by HCR to have criticised her poetry.

Beaumont, Sir George Howland (1753–1827) was a patron of the arts and landscape painter. He lived at Coleorton, Leicestershire (he lent his house to WW in 1806) and in Grosvenor Square, London. On first meeting, he took a dislike to STC, but then lodged next door to him at Keswick and fell under his spell. He offered WW land at Applethwaite in the Lake District to be near his friend. He helped STC to establish the *Friend* and, in later life, procure a pension. He was largely responsible for establishing the National Gallery. In his last years he may have become disillusioned with STC, as in his will he left Mrs C £50 and STC nothing (but see next entry).

Beaumont, Margaret, Lady (née Willes) (?–1829) married Sir George Beaumont in 1778. 'She is a deep enthusiast, sensitive, trembles and cannot keep the tears in her eye . . . you may wind her up with any music' (STC in letter to WW, 1803). In her will she left STC £50.

Beddoes, Dr Thomas (1760–1808) was a physician. He set up the Pneumatic Institute at Clifton, Bristol (where he employed the young Humphrey Davy). A convinced radical, he wrote anti-Pitt pamphlets. He supported STC in founding the *Watchman*, and corresponded with him about opium addiction. His sudden death upset STC greatly: 'Dr Beddoes' death has taken more Hope out of my Life, than any event I can remember' (letter to Montagu, 1819).

Betham, Mary Mathilda (1776–1852), a miniature painter, painted Mrs C and daughter Sara. STC wrote a poem to her, dated 9 September 1802.

Bowles, William Lisle (1762–1850) was a poet, divine and antiquary. STC was greatly influenced by his *Sonnets* (1789) while he was at Christ's Hospital. He was in turn Rector of Chicklade, Wiltshire, and of Dumbleton, Gloucestershire, then Vicar of Bremhill, Wiltshire, where he constructed his well-known garden. STC eventually made his acquaintance and stayed with him at Bremhill, writing comments on Bowles's poetry, during his year with the Morgans at Calne in 1815.

Bowyer, Reverend James (also spelt **Boyer**) (1736–1814) was Upper Master at Christ's Hospital. He had been educated there and at Balliol. There is a detailed description of him in Lamb's 'Christ's Hospital Five-and-thirty Years Ago' in *Essays of Elia*, and STC also sketched his character in *BL* (Biographical Supplement). He kept a *Liber Aureus* of boys' work he admired; STC appears in it several times. Despite his severity, STC wrote gratefully of him in *BL*.

Buller, Francis (*later* Sir Francis) (1746–1800) was the third son of James (below), a pupil of John Coleridge, and boarded with the family at Ottery. He became the youngest-ever judge in 1778 at the age of 32. As Judge Buller, he procured for STC a Presentation at Christ's Hospital.

Buller, James, of Downes, near Crediton, Devon, is supposed to have been the 'kind gentleman' who befriended John Coleridge on his father's bankruptcy and set him up as a schoolmaster. He settled eventually at Morval in Cornwall.

Burnett, George (1776–1811), the son of a well-to-do Somerset farmer, was refused by Martha Fricker. He was deeply committed to Pantisocracy and became its 'waif'. He could not settle to any profession, becoming Unitarian minister, army surgeon, hack writer. John Rickman (*q.v.*) gave him work on the census. He took to opium, and later abused STC and Southey as the cause of his downfall. He died miserably in the workhouse in Marylebone at the age of 35.

Caldwell, George was STC's 'earliest friend' at Jesus College, Cambridge. Later, he became a Fellow and Tutor at Jesus. He was still in touch with STC in 1813.

Cary, Henry Francis (1772–1844), scholar and translator, who translated *The Divine Comedy* in 1814. It was highly praised by STC, who persuaded Taylor and Hessey to publish a second edition in 1819. He met STC at Littlehampton in 1817 and became a friend.

Carlyon, Clement, MD (1777–1864), an English physician and traveller, met STC in Hanover in 1799 and travelled in his party on the expedition to the Brocken. He accompanied him as far as Brunswick on his way home. Later, he and George Greenhough (*q.v.*) published their own account of the trip. He published four volumes of *Early Years and Late Reflections* (1836–58), which are valuable for their insights into STC, Humphrey Davy and others.

Chester, John, was a farmer from Nether Stowey. A great admirer of STC, he was his companion on the trip to Germany (1798) and studied German agriculture on the journey.

Clarkson, Catherine (née Buck) (1772–1856) was a childhood friend of Crabb Robinson, whom he introduced to STC, CL and WW. She married Thomas Clarkson (see next entry). One of DW's closest friends, she was also for a time very close to STC, who thought of her in 1811 as a twin sister: 'She has all that is good in me, and all that is innocent' (Letter to HCR, 12 March 1811). However, she became embroiled in the quarrel with WW, grew disillusioned with STC after attempting in vain to persuade him to return north and seems to have faded from his life after 1813.

Clarkson, Thomas (1760–1846), reformer and vice-president of the Anti-slavery Society, lived at Eusemere near Penrith. He and his wife (see previous entry) moved to Bury St Edmunds in 1807. STC was a visitor there after his return from Malta.

Coleridge, David Hartley (1796–1849) was STC's first child. Adored by his father in childhood, he was written about by both STC and WW. Unworldly and vulnerable, he won a Fellowship to Oxford but lost it through drunken behaviour. He tried journalism and then became a schoolmaster in Ambleside, but for the last years of his life was something of a vagrant. In 1833 he published *Biographia Borealis* (lives of northern worthies) and *Sonnets*, and in 1840 editions of Massinger and Ford. He did not see his father for the last ten years of the latter's life. Befriended from childhood by the WWs, he is buried beside them at Grasmere.

Coleridge, Derwent (1800–83), the second son of STC, was very talented (particularly in languages) but was more balanced and capable than his brother Hartley (see entry above). In 1820, after a long wait, he eventually went to St John's, Cambridge, thanks to the generosity of some of STC's friends, particularly John Hookham Frere. After a period of atheism, he was ordained in 1825, happily married to Mary Pridham, and settled at Helston, Cornwall as a schoolmaster. In 1841 he became the first principal of St Mark's College, Chelsea. He edited Hartley's *Poems and Essays* after his death, and added a memoir (1849). After the death of his sister Sara (*q.v.*) he took over the editing of his father's works.

Coleridge, Edward (1800–83) was the youngest son of STC's eldest brother, James. He became a fellow of Eton and a regular visitor to STC at Highgate. With his brother Henry Nelson Coleridge (*q.v.*) he represented the family at STC's funeral.

Coleridge, Henry Nelson (1798–1843), a son of STC's eldest brother, James, was a barrister and author. He wrote *Six Months in the West*

Indies in 1825, and married STC's daughter Sara (*q.v.*) in 1829 after a long engagement. He recorded STC's *Table Talk* at Highgate. With his brother Edward he represented the family at STC's funeral, and was STC's literary executor, editing his father-in-law's works until his early death, when his wife took up the task.

Coleridge, John Taylor (1790–1876), the eldest son of STC's eldest brother, James, was a frequent visitor to STC at Highgate. He became a judge. His eldest son, John Duke Coleridge, was Lord Chief Justice and became the first Baron Coleridge.

Coleridge, Sara (née Fricker) (1770–1845) married STC in 1795. She bore him four children: David Hartley (1796–1849, *q.v.*), Berkeley (1798–1799), Derwent (1800–83, *q.v.*) and Sara (1802–52, *q.v.*), and coped with his frequent absences and their eventual separation with relative equanimity. When Southey moved into Greta Hall during STC's absence in Malta in 1804 she became part of his household. She spent her last years in the London home of her daughter Sara and son-in-law Henry Nelson Coleridge (*q.v.*). Her confidant and support was Thomas Poole. Her letters to him, which convey the flavour of her life as STC's wife, are published as *Minnow Among Tritons* (ed. Stephen Potter). STC was proud to stand with her in 1832 at the christening of their grandchild, Edith: he respected her but could not live with her. (See also **Fricker family.**)

Coleridge, Sara (1802–52) was STC's only daughter; a sylph-like creature as a child, a scholar as an adult. Brought up by her uncle, Robert Southey, she married her cousin, Henry Nelson Coleridge (*q.v.*) in 1829. She published: *Account of the Abipones,* translated from the Latin (1822); a translation of *Memoirs of the Chevalier Bayard* (1825); *Pretty Lessons in Verse for Good Children* (1834); and *Phantasmion* (1837). There are many testaments to her saintly character.

Coleridge, William Hart (1789–1849), the only child of STC's brother, Luke, saw much of STC during the Highgate years, but STC felt he did not do enough to help Derwent Coleridge (*q.v.*) to a curacy. He became Bishop of Barbados and took his cousin Henry Nelson Coleridge (*q.v.*) on a visit there in 1825. He held the post very successfully for 16 years and died in Salston, near Ottery St Mary.

Cottle, Joseph (1770–1853) was a publisher in Bristol and a Unitarian. He was the brother of Amos Cottle, the antiquarian. His financial backing helped launch both STC and Southey and ensured that neither took up professions which would distract them from poetry. However, he and his brother Amos were the victims of the mockery of STC and his friends. Good-natured and simple-hearted, he was among the last to recognise STC's opium addiction. In 1814, when he did at last understand the problem, he tried to raise money from STC's supporters for a cure. When, in answer to a begging letter in 1815, he sent only £5, STC never wrote to him again. He published *Early Recollections* (1837) and *Reminiscences of Coleridge and Southey* (1847). Both are full of inaccuracies and exaggerate Cottle's own importance – but Kathleen Coburn feels he has been for too long the victim of critical snobbery and deserves to be revalued.

Cruikshank, John was a friend of STC in Nether Stowey and land agent to Lord Egremont. He became treasurer of the group which supported STC with £35–40 a year after the collapse of the *Watchman*. In the early days at Stowey the Coleridges often visited the young Cruikshank family who had a little girl of Hartley's age.

Davy, Humphrey (*later* Sir Humphrey) (1778–1829), chemist, science lecturer and poet, went to Bristol in 1798 to work for Dr Beddoes (*q.v.*) at the Pneumatic Institute and met STC there. 'I never met such an extraordinary young man', said STC. Later, he arranged for STC to give lectures at the Royal Institution in London. In 1820 he succeeded Sir Joseph Banks (*q.v.*) as President of the Royal Society.

Dawe, George (1781–1829), portrait painter and mezzotint engraver, painted STC (and Godwin, Wellington *et al.*). He visited STC in the Lake District in 1812. He was a modest man; STC did not think much of his talents.

Dyer, George (1755–1841) was an eccentric poet and scholar. With CL, he provides one of the few links between STC's early and later life. Older than STC at Christ's Hospital, they met for the first time in London. He was interested in Pantisocracy. After the failure of the *Watchman*, he volunteered to pay off the outstanding printer's bills (£80 or £90). STC invited him to the Thursday evening Highgate gatherings. 'GD's character – moral (not intellectual). Truth and benevolence struggling' (*Notebooks*, I. 487).

Estlin, John Prior (1747–1817), a Unitarian minister and schoolmaster in Bristol, met STC there *c*.1795. He replaced John Cruikshank (*q.v.*) as treasurer of the fund set up to help STC after the *Watchman* closed. An eminent teacher and 'fine generous character', he was awarded an honorary degree from Glasgow University in 1807. He attended STC's lectures in Bristol in 1814 and quarrelled with him over a description of Satan in *Paradise Lost*.

Evans family Mrs Evans, a widow, lived with her children, Mary, Ann, Elizabeth and Tom, in Villiers Street, off the Strand, in London. Tom was befriended by STC, his senior, when he went to Christ's Hospital, and STC was in his turn befriended by the Evans family when he began to visit them *c*.1788. Mrs Evans acted as a mother-substitute and he fell in love with Mary. He did not dare declare his love till it was too late (see December 1794). Mary married Fryer Todd in October 1795 and was as unhappy in her marriage as STC in his. They met again briefly in 1808. Tom became a clerk in East India House.

Field, Reverend Matthew (1748–96) was Master of the Lower School at Christ's Hospital, and went on to Pembroke College, Cambridge, as a Fellow. Lamb and Leigh Hunt both describe him as easy-going and incompetent.

Frend, Reverend William (1757–1841), a tutor at Jesus College, Cambridge; mathematician, Unitarian and radical, was a great influence on the students, including STC. He was tried for blasphemy in 1794 and dismissed from the College.

Frere, John Hookham (1769–1846) was a diplomat and translator who became one of STC's close friends during the Highgate days, when they used to dine together at Blake's Hotel. He worked to procure a sinecure for STC in 1827; when this failed, he made him an annual gift of money so that he could take a holiday. STC spoke admiringly of him during his last years and in his will left notes of esteem to WW, RS and Frere. The will also describes Frere as, of all the men STC had known, the sweetest and kindest.

Fricker family The father was a Bristol manufacturer who died bankrupt in 1786, leaving his wife and six children (see entries below) penniless. Mrs Fricker set up a dress shop.

Fricker, Edith (1774–1837), a milliner, married Robert Southey in 1795. She lived at Greta Hall during STC's absence from 1804, but died insane.

Fricker, Eliza (1778–1868) was just a schoolgirl during the Pantisocratic years. She later had an affair with a sea captain and went to live on the Isle of Man.

Fricker, George (1785–1813) was generally regarded as a ne'er-do-well. Before going to Malta STC tried to find him a job. He later helped STC retrieve his papers from Customs after the Malta trip.

Fricker, Martha (1777–1850) rejected George Burnett's offer of marriage. She was a witness at STC's wedding. He always preferred her to her sisters and visited her when she was a struggling mantua-maker in London. She spent her last years with her sister Eliza on the Isle of Man. STC's daughter Sara described her and her sister Eliza as admirable women, earning their own living all their lives.

Fricker, Mary (1771–?1871), an actress, married Robert Lovell (*q.v.*) in 1794; after his early death in 1796 she was first looked after by STC and then in 1804 moved into Greta Hall with the Southeys during STC's absence in Malta. STC always found her a trial. She lived into her nineties.

Fricker, Sara see **Coleridge, Sara** (1770–1845).

Gillman, Dr James (1792–1839), a medical practitioner in Highgate, took STC into his house as a paying patient in 1816 and attempted to cure him of opium addiction. He and his wife looked after him loyally until his death eighteen years later. They built him a study and allowed him to set up the 'Thursday evenings' of conversation in their home. In return STC helped their sons James and Henry with their education and subsequent careers. STC praised them in his will and left them gifts. Gillman published a fairly inaccurate first volume of a *Life of Coleridge* in 1838 but died before he could complete the second volume.

Godwin, William (1756–1836), novelist, political philosopher and biographer, was the husband of Mary Wollstonecraft by whom he had a daughter Mary (later Mary Shelley). He met STC in London in

December 1799. They influenced each other's thinking over the years: STC modified his convictions towards theism; G said that STC had led him to a new appreciation of divinity in all its forms.

Green, Dr Joseph Henry (1791–1863) was Professor of Anatomy at the Royal Academy. STC made his acquaintance at Highgate. They used to dine together in Lincoln's Inn Fields. In 1818 he undertook to pay STC's annual insurance premium. He attended STC in his last illness: STC summoned him to his deathbed in order 'to leave you with the sole Depositorium of my mind'. G stayed with him during the night that he died, and in his will STC left G his property (his insurance policy worth £2560) and publishing rights in his manuscripts and letters, in trust for Mrs C and their children. G worked on STC's Opus Maximum for the rest of his life, but was not able to produce a coherent whole from the fragments. Gillman (*q.v.*) dedicated to Green his *Life of STC*.

Greenhough, George Bellas (1778–1855) was a geographer and geologist and an English traveller in Germany who met STC in Hanover in 1799. Later he and Clement Carlyon (*q.v.*) wrote reminiscences of their travels with STC. He met STC again in London while the latter awaited a ship for Malta in 1804. Later G became President of the Royal Geological Society.

Gutch, John Matthew (1776–1861) was at Christ's Hospital with STC. He moved to Bristol in 1803 where he became a journalist (he edited *Felix Farley's Bristol Journal*), a bookseller and a banker. With other former Christ's Hospital pupils he contributed to buying the manuscripts of the *Friend* in 1815. With William Hood (*q.v.*) he published two volumes of STC's poems in 1817. There were disputes with the author about overcharging. Later he published STC's *Essays* and the first part of *BL*. He preserved the notebook STC bought on arrival in Bristol in 1795 – hence it is known as the 'Gutch Notebook'.

Hamilton, Anthony was educated at St John's College, Cambridge. He met STC in Göttingen and took him to a German social club, the Saturday Club – much to STC's astonishment. On his return to England he took to the Wedgwoods, at STC's request, a commissioned pastel portrait of STC by a local Göttingen artist.

Hood, William, a friend of STC's from Bristol days, published with J. M. Gutch (*q.v.*), two volumes of STC's poetry in 1815.

Hucks, Joseph, an undergraduate of Cambridge University, accompanied STC on his walking tour of Wales in 1794. 'A man of cultivated, tho' not vigorous understanding', said STC. H later published *A Pedestrian Tour in North Wales* (1795) and a volume of poems (including one to STC) in 1798.

Hutchinson family consisted of the nine orphaned children of a farmer in County Durham (another child died in infancy). When STC first met them in 1799 they were living at Sockburn Hall Farm on a bend of the River Tees, the girls housekeeping for their brothers. This pattern continued throughout their lives, the family closeness being preserved by frequent visits. In addition to the children detailed in the entries below there were also: Elizabeth (1776–1832), Joanna (1780–1843) and William (1783–5).

Hutchinson, George (1778–1864) left Sockburn in 1800 for a new farm at Bishop Middleham, near Durham. STC visited him there with Sara H.

Hutchinson, Henry (1769–1834) was pressganged in 1818. STC worked for his release.

Hutchinson, John (1768–1833) was a businessman.

Hutchinson, Margaret (Peggy) (1772–96) may have been WW's Lucy.

Hutchinson, Mary (1770–1859) was at school at Penrith with DW; they became close friends. She married WW in 1802.

Hutchinson, Sara (1775–1835) was STC's 'Asra'. Her unconsummated love-affair with him developed until the collapse of the *Friend* in 1810. After this she left for her brother Thomas's (*q.v.*) new farm in North Wales. STC's quarrel with the WWs in 1811 meant that, on her return, although she spent much of the rest of her life with the WWs, she saw little of STC. There may have been plans for her to marry WW's brother John (*q.v.*). She died unmarried.

Hutchinson, Thomas (1773–1849) left Sockburn in 1800 for a new farm at Gallow Hill, near Scarborough. STC visited him there with Sara H. In 1810 he moved to Hindwell Farm, Radnorshire, North Wales, with his cousin, John Monkhouse (*q.v.*).

Klopstock, Friedrich Gottlieb (1724–1803) was a German poet and author of patriotic odes who introduced Shakespeare and Old Nordic and Celtic poets into the German Revival. STC thought of him as the father of German poetry, but when he and WW met him on their German tour in Hamburg in 1799 he found him 'disappointing'.

Le Grice, Charles Valentine (1773–1858) was a contemporary of STC at Christ's Hospital; they became friends at Cambridge (Le Grice was at Trinity College). He has left descriptions of evenings with STC discussing Burke's pamphlets and contemporary political events. He became a clergyman and settled in Penzance. In 1833 he met STC again at the British Association meeting in Cambridge and wrote an account of his sayings there. He published 'College Reminiscences' of STC and Lamb in the *Gentleman's Magazine* in 1833 and 1834.

Lloyd, Charles (1775–1839), a poet, stayed with STC and his family at Nether Stowey until his epileptic attacks made this impossible. He became estranged from STC after the publication of *Edmund Oliver* (1788) in which the central character is a cruel parody of his friend. After his marriage he moved to Ambleside and remained in touch with the WWs. A superficial reconciliation was affected with STC. L later went to France, where he died insane.

Longman, Thomas Norton (1771–1842) was a publisher. The publishing house of Joseph Cottle (*q.v.*) was bought by Longman and Rees *c.*1800 who thereby became the owners of the copyright of *Lyrical Ballads*. Longman, not considering them valuable, presented the copyright to Cottle, who in turn returned it to WW. Longman published the third edition of STC's *Poems* in 1803.

Lovell, Robert (1770–96) was a poet from a Bristol Quaker family. He was at Balliol with Southey and became one of the Pantisocratic group. He married Mary Fricker (*q.v.*) in 1794 and in the same year published poems with RS. He disapproved of STC's marriage to Sara Fricker (*q.v.*). He contributed to the *Watchman* and seemed destined for a successful career as a writer, but died of a fever at the age of 26, leaving a widow and child. Mrs Lovell later moved into Greta Hall with the Southeys.

Mackintosh, Sir James (1765–1832) was a lawyer and a London Scot. After the death of his first wife, the sister of Daniel Stuart (*q.v.*), he married a Wedgwood. He met STC through the Wedgwoods at Cote House near Bristol (home of John Wedgwood, brother of Josiah and Thomas); and beat STC in debate. A writer on philosophical matters, like STC he moved away from the early Radicalism. He visited Greta Hall. STC, always wary of him, found him 'without emotions'.

Middleton, Thomas Fanshawe (1769–1822) was a senior boy at Christ's Hospital. He introduced STC to Bowles's *Sonnets* and is supposed to have brought STC to the notice of Bowyer. Later, he went to Pembroke, Cambridge, where he failed to get a Fellowship, but became a clergyman, an editor and a poet and eventually Bishop of Calcutta. Gillman describes him as STC's 'Pole Star' in school. A Coleridge Memorial Prize, still awarded at Christ's Hospital, consists of a statuette of STC, Lamb and Middleton.

Monkhouse, John, was a cousin of the Hutchinsons. He was a farmer, and in 1810 went to Wales to share a farm with Tom Hutchinson (*q.v.*) at Hindwell in Radnorshire. Sara H (*q.v.*) accompanied him. By 1814 he was widowed and living with his married sister.

Monkhouse, Thomas (1783–1875), the brother of John (see above) and a cousin of the Hutchinsons (*qq.v.*), was a London merchant who lived at 34 Gloucester Place. He was famous for his literary dinners. At one particularly memorable one, on 4 April 1823, STC, WW, Lamb, Rogers and HCR were present and STC was 'in his finest vein of talk'. Mary Lamb referred to TM's daughter as 'a very pleasing girl', 'rather like Sara Hutchinson'. TM declined in health in 1824, went to Torquay, then to Clifton, where he died on 26 February 1825.

Montagu, Basil (1770–1851), barrister and author, was called to the Bar in May 1798. He was a friend of WW, through whom he met STC, probably in 1797. He married three times, the third time in 1808, and in 1810 precipitated the quarrel between STC and WW by indiscreet remarks. Later he and STC were reconciled and he visited

STC several times at Highgate (introducing Thomas Carlyle to him). STC left him a mourning ring in his will.

Morgan, John James (?1775–1820) was a school friend of Southey at Williams' School in Bristol. He came from a Unitarian family and met STC in early Bristol days. In 1810 he came to his rescue after the quarrel with WW, and thereafter stood by him during the worst stages of his opium addiction. STC lived for 18 months with the Morgan family at Ashley, near Bath, and then Calne, in Wiltshire, from 1814. John had become bankrupt in 1813. RS, CL and other friends raised an annuity for his benefit but he was soon in financial trouble again. He died after a stroke in 1820. STC and other friends continued to help his widow, Mary, and unmarried sister-in-law, Charlotte Brent.

Moxon, Edward (1801–58) was a publisher and poet. Samuel Rogers (*q.v.*), the banker-poet, helped to set him up in business with a loan of £500. In 1830 he published Charles Lamb, then STC and later Tennyson and Browning.

Murray, John (1778–1843) was a publisher who was involved with the *Edinburgh Review*, and then set up the *Quarterly Review* on Tory principles, in opposition to it. He maintained a close publishing association with Byron, on whose recommendation he published 'Christabel' in 1816. A rift with STC in 1817 over the publishing rights to *Zapolya* was never properly healed.

Parry, Charles and Frederick, were brothers of the Arctic explorer Sir William Parry. STC met them in Göttingen on the German tour in 1798. Their father was a famous physician, Caleb Hillier Parry. In 1814 he treated STC in Bath for the consequences of opium addiction.

Pinney, John was a rich Bristol sugar merchant. He and his brother Azariah became friends of the WWs; STC and WW first met at his house, 7 Great George Street, Bristol, in September 1795. He let Racedown in Dorset rent-free to WW, which caused trouble when his father found out. WW had to move on to Alfoxden in 1797. When planning to winter abroad (1801–2), STC at first considered borrowing the Pinney house at Nevis in the West Indies.

Poole, Thomas (1765–1837) was a well-to-do tanner of Nether Stowey. STC took Southey to meet him in July 1794. He supported STC thereafter at every stage of his life; he found him a cottage at Stowey adjoining his own garden, helped financially with the *Watchman* and the *Friend*, contributed to Hartley's education and wrote regularly to Mrs C. In his will STC left a mourning ring to Poole. See *Thomas Poole and His Friends*, by Mrs Henry Sandford, 2 vols, London: Macmillan, 1888.

Priestley, Joseph (1733–1804) was the scientist who discovered oxygen. A Birmingham Unitarian minister, his house was burnt down by the mob because he had welcomed the Fall of the Bastille. In 1773 he moved to Calne, Wiltshire, where he was librarian to Lord Shelburne (later first Marquis of Lansdowne) at Bowood and tutor to his sons. He remained there until 1780, when he returned to Birmingham. A dissenter, he emigrated to America in 1794. Southey and STC hoped for support from him for Pantisocracy. STC wrote a sonnet about him for the *Morning Chronicle* in 1794.

Rickman, John (1771–1840), a Parliamentary official, was a friend of Southey. He was secretary to the Speaker of the House of Commons, then promoted to second clerk assistant and eventually, in 1820, to chief clerk, a post he held until his death. STC met him at the Lambs' in 1803. He helped George Burnett, and was tolerant of STC's weaknesses: STC thought him 'a sterling man'.

Robinson, Henry Crabb (1775–1867) was a barrister and diarist. He was introduced to STC by his childhood friend Catherine Clarkson in London *c.*1810, and in 1812 helped to bring about a reconciliation between STC and WW after their quarrel. He gave many full accounts of STC, Lamb and the rest in his diaries; for example, of the famous dinner on 4 April 1823 at Thomas Monkhouse's (*q.v.*). STC saw him often during the Highgate years.

Robinson, Mary (Perdita) (1758–1800), an actress and fashionable beauty, was once mistress of the Prince Regent. She was one of STC's favourite 'literary ladies' in London from 1800. Perhaps her experience of opium may have influenced him. A few weeks before her death STC sent her 'A Stranger Minstrel'.

Rogers, Samuel (1763–1855) was a poet and banker who helped to set up Edward Moxon, the publisher (*q.v.*). He met STC *c.*1801 at Grasmere and later helped him by talking to the Prime Minister about a pension. STC seems to have had little respect for him or for his work.

Sharp, Richard (1759–1835), nicknamed 'Conversation' Sharp, was a businessman, MP and critic. He was a friend of Samuel Rogers (*q.v.*) whom he introduced to STC. STC always adopted a respectful tone in letters to S. In 1809 STC turned for help in paying for the *Friend* to S, with Tom Hutchinson, Poole and brother George Coleridge (only the last-named refused). S received the letter (24 April 1812) in which STC describes WW as 'my bitterest Calumniator' – and showed it to WW. This may have helped bring about the reconciliation in revealing to WW STC's state of mind.

Sotheby, William (1757–1833), poet, dramatist and translator, he became STC's staunch friend from their meeting in 1802. He received a series of long letters from STC dealing with his beliefs about poetry, including the distinction between 'imagination' and 'fancy', and revelations such as 'WW's Preface is half the child of my own brain'. He saw STC often during the Highgate years.

Sterling, John (1805–44) was one of STC's disciples in the Highgate years, immortalised in Thomas Carlyle's *Life of John Sterling*. He adored Coleridge during his lifetime, but a few years after his death wrote critically of his idleness and plagiarisms. He was probably influenced by Carlyle, whose own estimate of STC was consistently unfavourable, even though he had only met him briefly at Dr James Gillman's (*q.v.*) in 1824–5.

Stoddart, Sir John (1773–1856), a barrister and journalist, stayed at Greta Hall in 1800. He reviewed the second edition of *Lyrical Ballads* favourably. He was Judge Advocate in Malta, 1803–7, and gave STC an invitation to visit there, which prompted the Malta sojourn of 1804–6. His sister Sarah married William Hazlitt. STC quarrelled with him over his failure to recover STC's papers from Naples in 1808.

Stuart, Daniel (1766–1846) was a journalist, editor of the *Morning Post*, 1796–*c.*1802, and editor and owner of the *Courier*, 1803–11. He met STC through Sir James Mackintosh (*q.v.*) in 1797. STC's first lines appeared in the *Morning Post* on 7 December 1797; S paid him a guinea a week for his contributions. He moved to London to write for the *Courier* in 1806. S helped to pay for the *Friend*, but there was a misunderstanding about what he had offered and STC felt that S had let him down. In 1838 S wrote anecdotes of STC, WW and Lamb for the *Gentleman's Magazine*. *Letters from the Lake Poets to Daniel Stuart* was published privately in 1889.

Thelwall, John (1764–1834) was a poet and revolutionary. He studied divinity and law, and in 1794 was tried for high treason with Horne Tooke, Tom Hardy and Thomas Holcroft. All were acquitted after several weeks in the Tower of London. He stayed with STC at Stowey in 1797 and met WW and Lamb. His presence aroused local suspicion of a spy ring. In the following year he retired to Wales and became a lecturer in elocution, specialising in speech therapy.

Wade, Josiah, a linen-draper of Bristol and early friend of STC, was witness, with Martha Fricker, at STC's marriage at St Mary Redcliffe, Bristol, in 1795. He helped STC financially and practically over the *Watchman*. STC stayed with him at his house, 2 Queen's Square, Bristol, in 1813 in the depths of his opium addiction and W received his famous letter of repentance (26 June 1814): 'In the one crime of OPIUM, what crime have I not made myself guilty of!' In his will STC left W a mourning ring.

Wedgwood, Josiah, was the second son of Josiah Wedgwood senior (1730–95), the founder of the Staffordshire pottery firm, whom he succeeded in running the firm. He met STC at the home of his elder brother John, Cote House, near Bristol, probably in December 1797. With his brother Thomas (*q.v.*), in January 1798 he offered STC an annuity to enable him to write poetry, which avoided the necessity for STC to go into the ministry. When the firm lost money as a result of the Napoleonic Wars, he wrote in 1812 to ask to be honourably released from his agreement. This did not affect STC's affection for him.

Wedgwood, Thomas (1771–1805) was the third surviving son of Josiah Wedgwood senior and brother of Josiah (*q.v.*). An invalid, fond of science and philosophy, he is described in the *Dictionary of National Biography* as 'the first photographer'. He was attracted to

STC's conversation when he met him with Josiah in 1797. He planned to go abroad for his health with STC as companion in 1802, but rapidly declined and died of 'thickening of the gut' (probably stomach cancer) while STC was in Malta.

Wilkinson, Thomas, WW's Quaker friend, lived at Yanwath in the Lake District. In 1809 he was visited for a month by STC whom he kept 'without spirits'. The *Friend* was successfully launched on 1 June that year, and DW said: 'TW is the father of *The Friend*.'

Wilson, John (1785–1854), a wealthy and talented poet and sportsman, built a house at Elleray on Lake Windermere where STC and WW visited him. When he lost his fortune in 1811 he went to Edinburgh and became the foremost writer for *Blackwood's Magazine*. He may have been the author of a scathing review of *BL* in October 1817 and, under the pseudonym 'Christopher North', was the author of a savage attack on Tennyson's *Poems* of 1830. Later in life he befriended Hartley Coleridge.

Wordsworth, John (1772–1805) was WW's sailor-brother. STC met him on his first trip to the Lakes in 1799. When he was drowned in the sinking of the *Earl of Abergavenny* off Portland Bill STC was grief-stricken. At one point (in Malta) he wished he had died at sea instead of JW. This may have been because he believed that JW would have married Sara H.

Bibliography

Coleridge's own letters and notebooks, the subject of magnificent scholarly work in the last forty years, are the major source of information:

Collected Letters of Samuel Taylor Coleridge, ed. Earl Leslie Griggs, 6 vols, published in pairs, Oxford, 1956, 1959, 1971.

The Notebooks of Samuel Taylor Coleridge, ed. Kathleen Coburn, 3 vols, London, 1957, 1962, 1973.

The British Library in London holds Coleridge's original Notebooks, nos 1–50, Add. Mss. 47, 496–7, 545. It also possesses the Egerton papers, 2800–1; the Gutch Notebook, Add. Mss. 27091; and the papers of Thomas Poole, Add. Mss. 35, 343–5.

E. H. Coleridge's notes to his edition of the *Poetical Works*, 2 vols, Oxford, 1912, 1975, have provided useful bibliographical material, although some of his theories (for example, about the dating of 'Kubla Khan') have been overtaken by more recent research.

For Coleridge's prose works I have used the *Collected Works*, general eds Kathleen Coburn and Bart Winer, being published in the Bollingen series, Princeton, N.J.: Princeton University Press, 1972– .

Letters of Coleridge's family and friends have been frequently consulted:

Mrs Coleridge: *Minnow among Tritons*, ed. Stephen Potter, London, 1934; rept. New York: AMS Press, 1973.

Sara Coleridge (STC's daughter): *Memoir and Letters of Sara Coleridge*, ed. Edith Coleridge, 2 vols, 1873.

Sara Hutchinson: *The Letters of Sara Hutchinson*, ed. Kathleen Coburn, London, 1954.

Lamb: *The Letters of Charles and Mary Lamb*, ed. Edwin J. Marrs Jr, 3 vols, Ithaca, N.Y., 1975.

Southey: *New Letters of Robert Southey*, ed. Kenneth Curry, 2 vols, New York, 1965.

Dorothy Wordsworth: *Journals of Dorothy Wordsworth*, ed. Ernest de Selincourt, 2 vols, London, 1941.

William Wordsworth: *The Letters of William and Dorothy Wordsworth*, ed. Ernest de Selincourt, 8 vols, Oxford, 1935–9; the first six volumes have been consulted in the revised edition, 1967–82.

The following books by or about Coleridge's circle have been essential reading, though in the case of Cottle and Gillman they make very dubious history:

Cottle: Joseph Cottle, *Early Recollections: Chiefly Relating to the Late Samuel Taylor Coleridge*, 2 vols, 1837.

Crabb Robinson: *The Correspondence of Henry Crabb Robinson with the Wordsworth Circle*, ed. Edith J. Morley, 2 vols, Oxford, 1927; *Henry Crabb Robinson on Books and their Authors*, ed. Edith J. Morley, 3 vols, London, 1938.

De Quincey: *Thomas De Quincey: His Life and Writings*, ed. H. A. Page, 2 vols, 1877.

Frere: Gabrielle Festing, *John Hookham Frere and his Friends*, 1899.

Gillman: James Gillman, *The Life of Samuel Taylor Coleridge*, 1838.

Hazlitt: *William Hazlitt: Selected Writings*, ed. Ronald Blythe, London, 1987.

Poole: Mrs Henry Sandford, *Thomas Poole and His Friends*, 2 vols, 1888.

Biographies consulted:

Campbell, James Dykes, *Samuel Taylor Coleridge*, 1894; London: Basil Savage, 1970.

Chambers, E. K., *Samuel Taylor Coleridge: A Biographical Study*, Oxford, 1938.

Holmes, Richard, *Coleridge: Early Visions*, London, 1989.

Sultana, Donald, *Samuel Taylor Coleridge in Malta and Italy*, New York, 1969.

Watson, Lucy E., *Coleridge at Highgate*, London, 1925.

Whalley, George, *Coleridge and Sara Hutchinson*, London, 1955.

F.B. Pinion's *A Wordsworth Chronology* (London, 1988) has been invaluable throughout.

Index